Isles of Scilly

ROYAL CRUISING CLUB
PILOTAGE FOUNDATION
Robin Brandon
Revised by John and Fay Garey

Imray Laurie Norie & Wilson Ltd
St Ives Cambridgeshire England

Published by
Imray Laurie Norie & Wilson Ltd
Wych House St Ives Huntingdon
Cambridgeshire PE17 4BT England 1999
☎ +44 (0)1480 462114
Fax +44 (0)1480 496109
E-mail ilnw@imray.com.
Website http://www.imray.com

South England Pilot Volume V Isles of Scilly
Lt. Col. R. J. Brandon
1st edition 1980
2nd edition 1983
Isles of Scilly Pilot
3rd edition 1994

© Royal Cruising Club Pilotage Foundation 1999

ISBN 0 85288 411 7

British Library Cataloguing in Publication Data.
A catalogue record for this book is available from the British Library.

This work, based on surveys over a period of many years, has been corrected to February 1999 from sea and land-based visits to the ports and harbours of the coast, from contributions by visiting yachtsmen and from official notices. The most recent photographs were taken during the summer 1997.

CAUTION

Every effort has been made to ensure the accuracy of this book. It contains selected information and thus is not definitive and does not include all known information on the subject in hand; this is particularly relevant to the plans, which should not be used for navigation. The Royal Cruising Club Pilotage Foundation believes that this selection represents a useful aid to prudent navigation, but the safety of a vessel depends ultimately on the judgement of the navigator, who should assess all information, published or unpublished.

CORRECTIONS

The Royal Cruising Club Pilotage Foundation would be glad to receive any corrections, information or suggestions which readers may consider would improve the book. Letters should be addressed to the Editor, *Isles of Scilly*, care of the publishers.

CORRECTIONAL SUPPLEMENTS

This pilot book is amended at intervals by the issue of correctional supplements prepared by the Royal Cruising Club Pilotage Foundation. Supplements are supplied free of charge with the books when they are purchased. Additional supplements are also available free from the publishers' website or on receipt of a stamped, addressed A4 envelope and a note of the name of the book for which the supplement is required.

WAYPOINTS

The Pilotage Foundation considers that waypoints should not be included in the text. The reasons are straightforward.

First, the estimation of latitude and longitude may vary by more than a mile between disciplines and there are three disciplines to be considered at any one moment: that used in this volume, that employed on the chart used by the navigator and that programmed into the aid in use. Each discipline may require its own correction and it is unlikely that all three will be the same. Only the first can be known to the author.

Second, waypoints should be chosen in relation to prevailing conditions. Given the inherent inaccuracies of all navigational aids, a waypoint, safe and sensible when visibility is 10 miles, may be dangerous and foolhardy when visibility is 10 metres. The detailed positioning of a ship in relation to the land depends upon interpretation of all information available, including that received by eye, and it does no harm to remind the navigator of this. When conditions are such that no information can be received by eye, encouragement of a false sense of security by adherence to a specified but possibly misleading waypoint is likely to create more problems than it solves.

Positions given in the text and on plans are intended purely as an aid to locating the place in question on the chart, and unless otherwise specified use the same datum as the largest scale chart of the area currently available.

PLANS

The plans in this guide are not to be used for navigation. They are designed to support the text and should always be used with navigational charts.

Printed in Great Britain by
Galliards, Great Yarmouth.

Contents

Foreword

The Royal Cruising Club Pilotage Foundation was created by members of the RCC to enable them and others to bring their experience of sailing and cruising to a wider public and to encourage the aspiring sailor to cruise further afield with confidence.

The Pilotage Foundation is a registered charity whose object is 'to advance the education of the public in the science and practice of navigation'. It was established with a generous grant by an American member of the RCC, Dr Fred Ellis, and fulfils its remit by producing and maintaining pilot books and cruising guides. Present volumes range from the Baltic to the West Indies and from Greenland to the Rio Grande.

The Foundation is extremely grateful and privileged to have been given the copyrights to pilots written by a number of distinguished authors and yachtsmen, charged with the willingly accepted task of keeping the original books up to date. Amongst such authors was the late Robin Brandon, and this volume is the first of his to be updated by means of a new edition.

The Foundation is most grateful to John and Fay Garey for all their skilful work in producing what is clearly a worthy new edition of the original.

W H Batten
Chairman and Director
Royal Cruising Club Pilotage Foundation
April 1999

Acknowledgements

For their assistance in the preparation of this work, the editors wish to thank Jeff Penhaligon – harbourmaster, St Mary's; Bill Burrows and Steve Douglas – assistant harbourmasters, St Mary's; Henry Birch – harbourmaster, Tresco; Will Wagstaff – Island Wildlife Tours, St Mary's; Mike Nelhams – head gardener, Tresco Abbey Gardens; Jack Hopkins – Met. Office, Marine Consultancy Office; Chris Jenkins; Anthony Houlton, Charles Nodder and Dick Trafford.

Royal Cruising Club Pilotage Foundation pilots and guides

Published by Imray Laurie Norie & Wilson Ltd
Atlantic Spain and Portugal
Atlantic Islands
Islas Baleares
Mediterranean Spain – Costas del Sol & Blanca – Costas del Azahar, Dorada & Brava
The Baltic Sea
North Biscay
North Brittany
Channel Islands
Lesser Antilles – with SHOM
North Africa
Faroe, Iceland & Greenland
Chile

Published by A & C Black Ltd
Atlantic Crossing Guide
Pacific Crossing Guide

Published by RCC Desktop Publishing Unit
Cruising Guide to West Africa
The Falkland Islands Shores
The South Atlantic Coast of South America

I. Introduction

The islands referred to in this guide may be called The Scilly Isles, The Isles of Scilly or Scilly. They are never called 'the Scillies'.

Most UK-registered yachts arrive in the Isles of Scilly from nearby home ports in Cornwall or Devon, and their owners are making their annual pilgrimage to their favourite offshore islands. Perhaps the lack of British yachts from further afield is due to the substantial distance to Scilly from major yachting centres and to limitations on time available for the return passage. However, visiting yachtsmen who persevere with the trip to Scilly will be rewarded by some of the most beautiful scenery in all England, together with bird-life and flowers of an unrivalled nature.

In recent years there has been an abundance of foreign yachts, of which French-flag vessels account for about three-quarters of all visitors while Dutch, German, Belgian and Irish flags appear about equally among the other yachts.

Needless to say, the months of July and August bring the largest number of visitors, with the main weight of French yachts passing through in August. For many of the foreign-flag vessels, Scilly is only a staging post on the way to more distant destinations. For example, many French yachts are bound for southern Ireland: conversely Irish yachts are bound for the French coast.

Scilly lies about 28 miles from Land's End. This is not a great distance from the mainland and indeed Land's End can easily be seen from Scilly in clear weather. But the islands are out in the ocean and until earlier this century even the tax man was not prepared to force his attentions on the inhabitants. From Redruth in Cornwall income tax was assessed on Scilly dwellers but no effort was made to enforce collection. If, before the arrival of air transport, the tax man did not wish to attempt the passage to Scilly by boat, he was probably also influenced by the lack of protected harbours when he arrived.

Scilly is not a suitable area for the inexperienced yachtsman. The approach can be subject to severe weather with little advance warning, while visibility can also be suddenly reduced. There are strong and sometimes unpredictable tidal streams in the offing. There are few lights and buoys and many tricky unmarked dangers. No anchorage offers 100% protection from wind and sea, and when the wind changes it may be necessary to move elsewhere in difficult conditions.

However, Scilly presents no more difficulty than many other destinations around Britain. A well-found yacht is necessary, together with up-to-date charts of the area and approaches, and appropriate navigational aids and publications. An auxiliary engine in good working order is a must.

Otherwise, the essential factor is a careful study beforehand of the approaches both from charts and from photographs, together with accurate note-taking about tidal streams, tide times and heights, and daymarks and lights likely to be met in the approaches. Scilly is just the place to test your abilities in demanding, yet beautiful surroundings.

Most sailing vessels visiting Scilly are fin-keel yachts, although there is a fair sprinkling of twin-keel vessels, catamarans and trimarans. Enterprising fin-keelers who have brought legs to enjoy one or two of the many shallow harbours are occasionally seen.

This guide examines the all-tide anchorages where a yacht drawing around 1·8m may be always afloat and where space exists for more than four or five vessels. Most of the other anchorages (many are little more than coves) suffer from one or more of the following disadvantages:

1. They are too shallow and either cannot be entered in a fin-keel yacht or the time available for remaining afloat at anchor is short.
2. The holding is poor. Heavy growth of weed makes some coves virtually impassable.
3. Their situation offers little or no shelter in bad weather and a quick departure might be difficult.

There are some other all-tide anchorages which are given consideration. These anchorages suffer from certain disadvantages such as, for example, that they offer little or no shelter from more than moderate seas or winds or they have only limited room for a few yachts.

This guide also includes a selection of small coves which, despite their disadvantages, skilled yachtsmen may wish to enter in shoal-draught craft in settled weather.

In addition to anchorages and their facilities, details of the islands' history are included, together with some facts about the birds, animals and flowers to be found in this Atlantic Arcadia.

Pilotage in the Isles of Scilly

It is best to arrange the final approach to Scilly so as to allow enough time to anchor in daylight. All other arrangements and plans for making a visit to Scilly should be made with this in mind. Because the islands are so low – with no land higher than 46 metres – the recognition of visual marks is especially important. For this reason navigators should carry,

St Agnes old lighthouse, looking NExN across St Mary's
Sound

and be prepared to use, an accurate hand-bearing compass, a good pair of binoculars and up-to-date large-scale charts. With such basic equipment, competent navigators can do without electronic aids when sailing in and around Scilly, although no doubt a depth gauge and a radar set are helpful in these waters, and a GPS set may be useful offshore.

The seamen of Scilly have themselves long used daymarks and transits for navigation and, in conditions where strong winds and tides often prevail, such immovable objects are reliable navigational tools. Eyeball navigation not only enables one to check position fixes obtained electronically, but also aids recognition of and familiarity with the geography, both of which are fundamental to safe pilotage.

There is a lot of shoal water among the islands, and submerged rocks and sandbanks are everywhere. Fortunately, the area is well charted but many of the hazards are not marked by buoys or beacons and may only be visible at LW.

The golden rule when sailing among the islands is to do so on a flood tide, ideally after half tide. However, individual yachtsmen must make their own assessment of conditions, as barometric pressure, among other factors, can have a great affect on sea level.

Another point to bear in mind when navigating

among these islands is: 'never follow the ferries'; they are so shallow-draught they can almost cross dry land!

So let us look first at the most useful fixed navigational marks. There are two tall well-maintained and brightly painted daymarks in Scilly: one is the old white lighthouse building on St Agnes (49m) and the other is the red and white horizontally banded daymark (56m) at the NE end of St Martin's. Because of their colouring and position, one or both of these unlit marks can, in reasonable visibility, be seen on many approaches to Scilly and they show up more readily in binoculars than less conspicuous objects. They are most helpful in approaches from S and E when both offer position checks by compass. These two marks have been carefully preserved since the 1680s and testify to the trust which mariners have placed in them for over 300 years. By contrast, the charted high marks on St Mary's – notably the TV tower, the latticed Decca masts and the grey telegraph tower – can be curiously indistinguishable at a distance, particularly against a background of cloud, although the TV tower can be a useful part of transit lines when navigating among the islands. There is also a daymark (43m) on top of Watch Hill, Bryher (see photo page 5), but unfortunately it is less brightly painted than those on St Agnes and St Martin's. This mark needs to be observed well before closing the coast as it disappears under the high ground of

The prominent daymark on the E end of St Martin's

Shipman Head. Nonetheless, the mark does offer those arriving from N or NW a useful check on their position during the approach.

The daymark on Watch Hill (Bryher), looking W of S from above Cromwell's Castle (Tresco)

TV tower

Decca masts

Telegraph tower

Transits and bearings of reference

Transits are widely used in this guide and the importance of steering to offset leeway and tidal streams when using transits cannot be overemphasised. Never leave an inexperienced person on the helm to look over their shoulder at a stern transit in a strong cross tide! In Scilly they will soon find the bottom.

The importance of arriving in Scilly in daylight has already been emphasised, and it should be equally stressed that a passage to these islands should never be attempted in bad weather. Yachts lying snugly in mainland harbours should stay where they are if fog or gales are forecast. If already en route to the islands, one should not try to enter them in gale conditions. Strong winds from any direction, superimposed on the almost everlasting swell from the Atlantic, are a recipe for trouble in the narrow, tidal, rocky sounds.

Great Cheese Rock

TV tower

Crow Rock Bn

Looking on a bearing of 160° on the transit of Crow Rock beacon with the TV tower (N St Mary's) (line S)

Swells from the Atlantic, are a recipe for trouble in the narrow, tidal, rocky, sounds.

Remember too that the islands are low and largely cliffless, and therefore radar echoes will not give a clear image of the shore – let alone of the off-lying rocks. In poor visibility – particularly fog – it is wise to stand off clear of the shipping lanes and await clearer conditions.

If caught out by a gale en route, the following courses of action are open, depending on the direction of the wind:

1. Heave-to clear of the shipping lanes and await better weather.
2. Proceed to Mount's Bay and take shelter in Newlyn or Penzance. (Note that the dock gate in Penzance Inner Harbour entrance only opens between HW −1½ hours and HW).
3. Proceed to St Ives Bay and anchor.
4. Proceed to Cork harbour in SE Ireland.

Measurements, bearings, distances and charts
Distances are given in sea miles (M) and occasionally in metres and decimetres. Soundings and drying heights are given in metres at Lowest Astronomical Tide (LAT) and elevations (in metres) are given as above the level of Mean High Water Springs (MHWS). Bearings are True and the 360 degree notation is used. Directional safety is shown using cardinal and sub-cardinal points, and bearings and directions are from seaward.

In this publication the charts referred to in connection with pilotage at Scilly are Admiralty charts no. *34* and no. *883*. These charts should be standard equipment on visiting yachts and it is suggested that readers refer to them while reading this guide.

Meteorology

The Isles of Scilly have the most unpredictable and rapidly changing weather conditions. The prudent skipper will obtain every forecast available and will keep a radio and visual watch for gale warnings. A careful watch should also be kept on the barometer for indications of deteriorating weather despite what the weather forecasts predict. In unsettled weather secondary depressions may form to the W of the islands and quickly produce a very rough sea.

Winds
Winds are mainly from the W, with winds from NW, SW and N the next most common. SE winds are the least frequent, as the wind roses show (opposite). Light sea breezes are sometimes a feature during warm fine summer afternoons and weak land breezes may be found at night.

Gales
There are more gales the further W along the S coast of England one proceeds. The average frequency of gales a month is as follows:

Jan	*Feb*	*Mar*	*Apr*	*May*	*Jun*	*Jul*	*Aug*	*Sep*	*Oct*	*Nov*	*Dec*
4·7	2·8	2·6	1·4	1·1	0·1	0·4	0·6	1·4	2·3	3·5	5·7

They are usually associated with deep depressions moving within 400M. Wind speeds of 90 knots have been recorded, but this is very exceptional, the usual maximum wind speed being between 34 and 47 knots (Beaufort force 8–9).

Clouds
The average cloud cover is 5 to 6 octas (eighths) throughout the year, showing a slight improvement in the afternoon in the area of the Isles of Scilly.

Precipitation
Snow, hail and sleet are included with rain. There are considerable yearly and monthly variations, which can make nonsense of the averages given below. The greatest amount of rain occurs with the passage of a front and during thunderstorms.

	No. of days 1mm+	*Amount* mm
January	16·3	95
February	12·4	79
March	12·2	73
April	9·3	48
May	9·7	58
June	8·2	48
July	9·2	54
August	9·6	64
September	11·2	69
October	12·2	82
November	14·7	96
December	15·8	97

Snow
Snow and sleet can fall on the islands at any time between November and April, but the average is 4·4 days a year between January and March. Snow lies 0·5 days a year measured at 0900 hours.

Thunderstorms
Thunderstorms usually form over France at the end of a period of fine weather and drift across the Channel to affect this area.

Fog and visibility
Sea fog can occur at any time when a warm moist airstream crosses a colder mass of water. This usually occurs as a SW–W warm sector airstream approaches this coast; it is most frequent in early summer. Land fog can also occur on cold still nights and days and may drift across the coastline. On the mainland the average is one day of fog a month during the summer months and two to three days a month during the winter. The reverse applies to the area of the Isles of Scilly.

Air temperature
The average daily maximum temperature is 19·2°C in August and 9·0°C in February. The average daily minimum temperatures in these months are 13·7°C and 2·6°C, respectively.

Relative humidity
The relative humidity can vary from 100% in rain and fog to about 40% in a dry NE airstream in summer. The average is around 90% at night in winter and around 75% at mid-day in the summer.

Oceanography

Sea surface temperatures

The sea is at its coldest towards the end of February and warmest during August, as follows:

Feb	May	Aug	Nov
9·7°C	11·4°C	16·3°C	12·7°C

Seas

The seas in this area can range from rough (2m) to very high (9m) in strong winds created by deep depressions; they are rarely completely calm.

Swell

The area is subject to swell from the SW–W. During the winter there is a swell of over 4m in height on average 10 days a month.

Sea level

Sea level can depart from predicted tidal levels due to strong winds or unusually high or low barometric pressure. Low pressure of 960mb can raise the sea level by about 0·5m over the predicted level and high pressure of 1040mb can lower the sea level by about 0·3m. Wind-induced surges in the Scilly area are likely to be much smaller than those affecting the coastal areas of the central Irish Sea or eastern England, and are unlikely to exceed 0·5m.

Currents

Currents are created on the surface of the sea by prevailing and recent winds. They run in a direction of about 30° to the right of the wind and their speed is related to the strength of the wind and its duration, being about 1/30th of the wind speed. These currents are most prevalent in winter between November and January, with a frequency of about 9% of the time and a speed of 1 to 2 knots. In summer, from May to July, they only occur for 1% of the time.

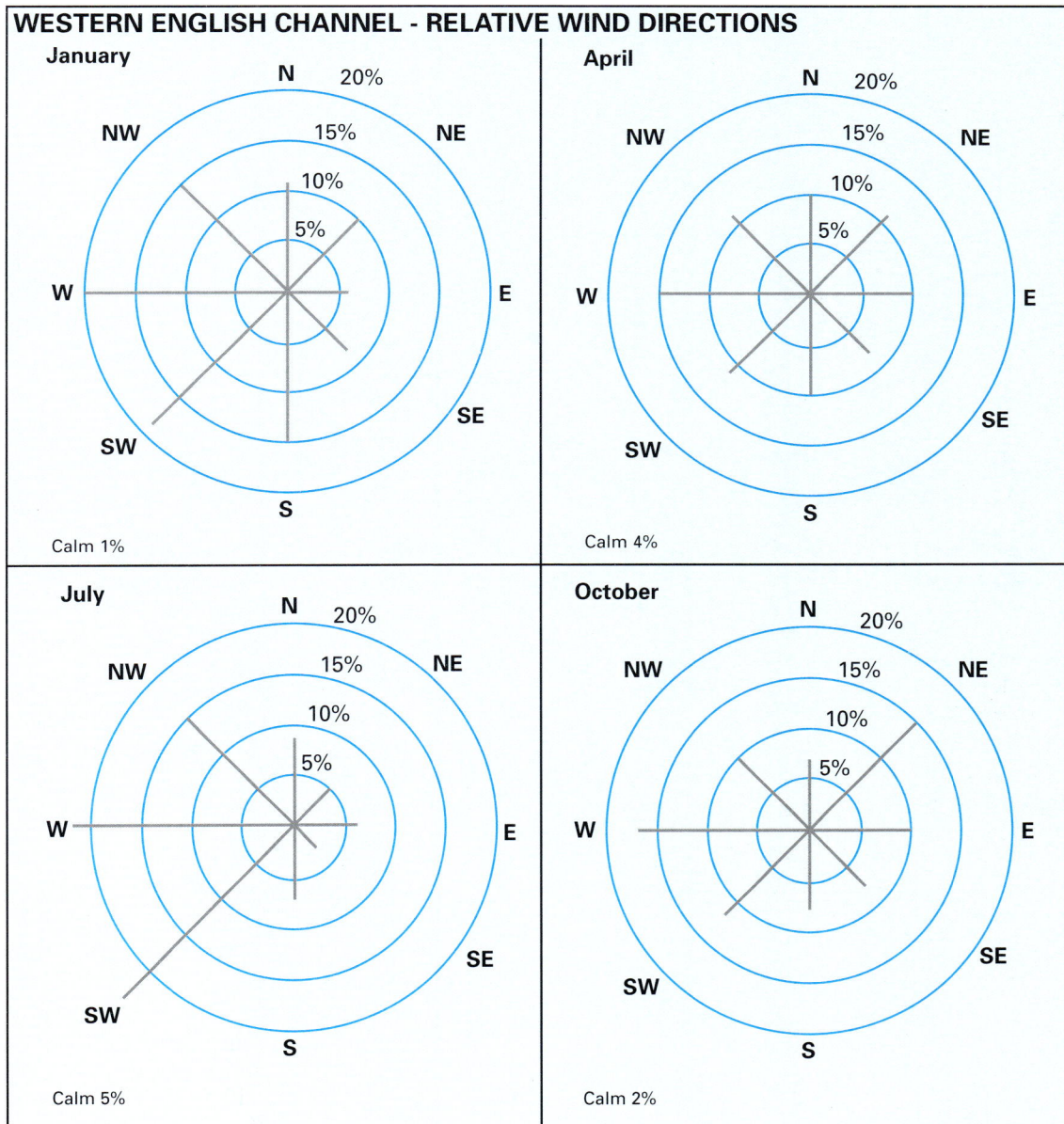

WESTERN ENGLISH CHANNEL - RELATIVE WIND DIRECTIONS

January — Calm 1%

April — Calm 4%

July — Calm 5%

October — Calm 2%

TIDAL STREAMS – ISLES OF SCILLY

Note: figures refer to mean rates in knots at neaps and springs; thus 03,05 indicates 0.3 Knots (neaps) and 0.5 Knots (Springs)

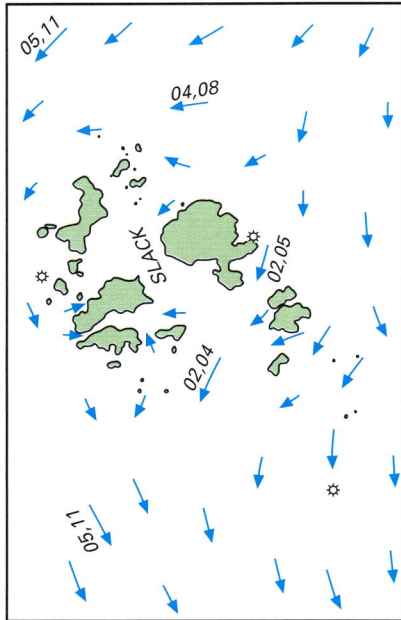

07,14
05,11
03,05
01,03

0500 BEFORE HW DEVONPORT
0405 BEFORE HW ST MARY'S

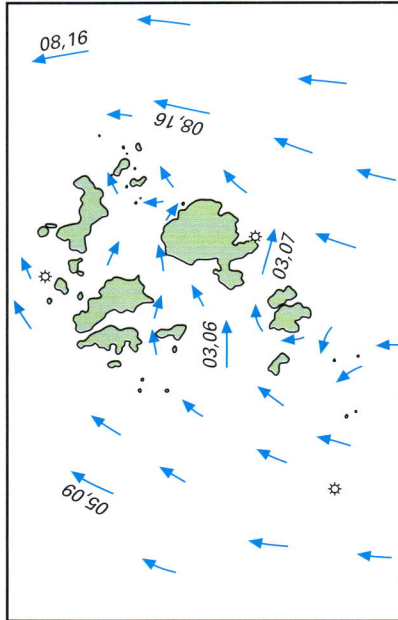

08,16
08,17
05,12
04,10
08,16

0300 BEFORE HW DEVONPORT
0205 BEFORE HW ST MARY'S

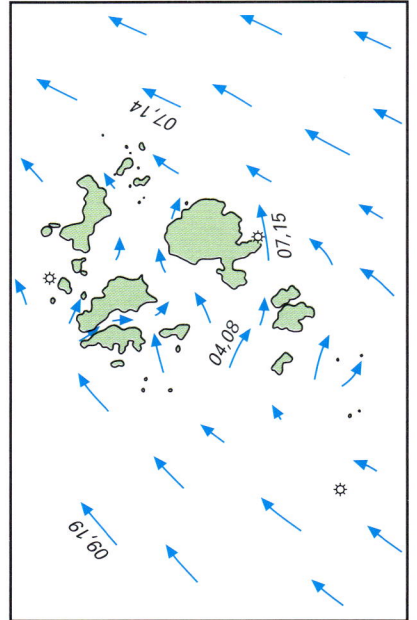

05,11
04,09
08,17
03,07
08,16

0100 BEFORE HW DEVONPORT
0005 BEFORE HW ST MARY'S

05,11
04,08
SLACK
02,05
02,04
05,11

0600 BEFORE HW DEVONPORT
0505 BEFORE HW ST MARY'S

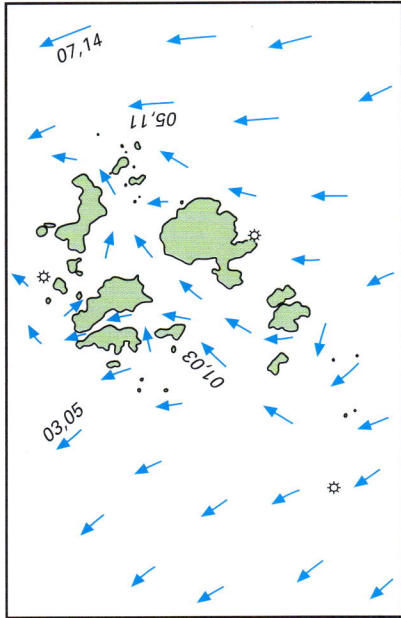

08,16
08,16
03,07
03,06
05,09

0400 BEFORE HW DEVONPORT
0305 BEFORE HW ST MARY'S

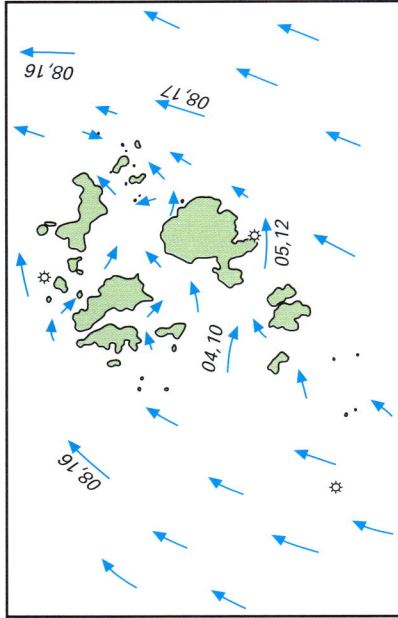

07,14
07,15
04,08
09,19

0200 BEFORE HW DEVONPORT
0105 BEFORE HW ST MARY'S

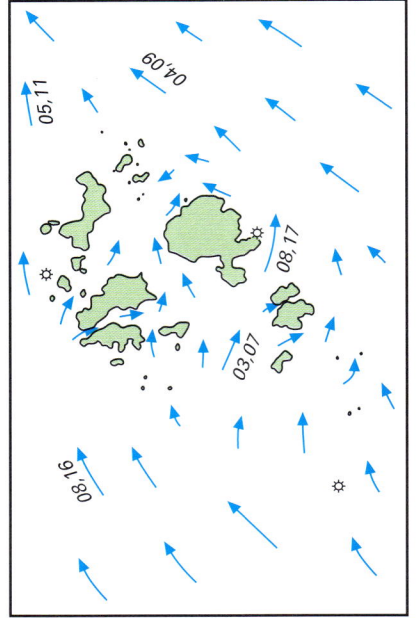

0100 AFTER
HW DEVONPORT
0105 AFTER
HW ST MARY'S

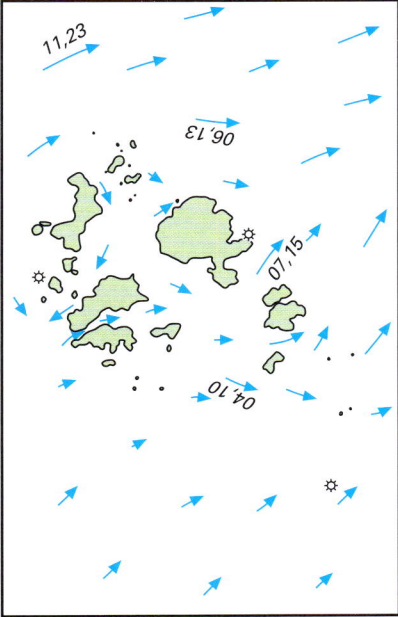

0300 AFTER
HW DEVONPORT
0355 AFTER
HW ST MARY'S

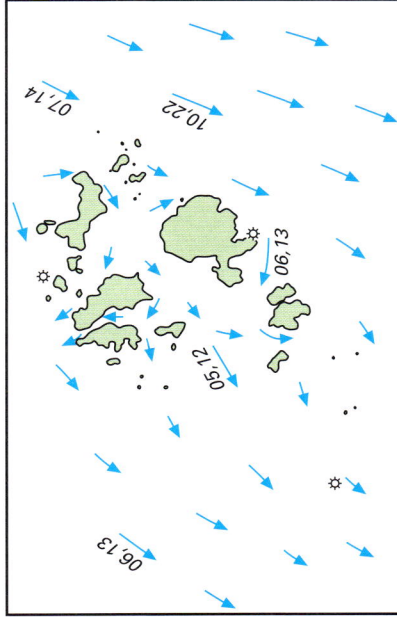

0500 AFTER
HW DEVONPORT
0555 AFTER
HW ST MARY'S

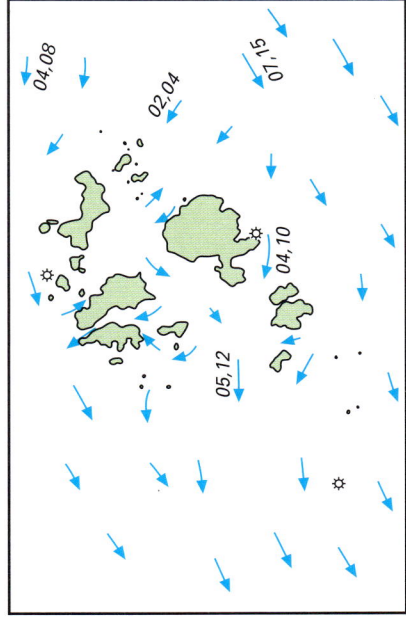

HW DEVONPORT
0055 AFTER
HW ST MARY'S

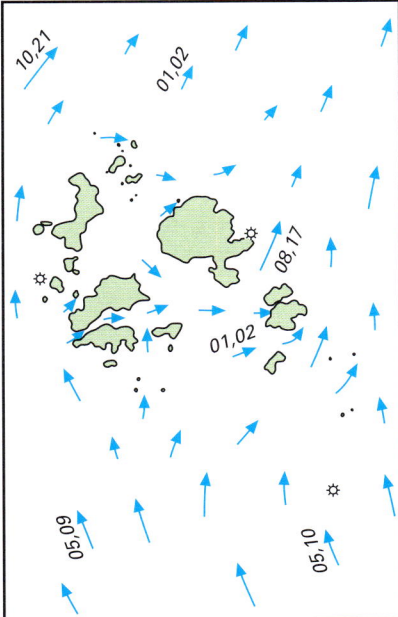

0200 AFTER
HW DEVONPORT
0255 AFTER
HW ST MARY'S

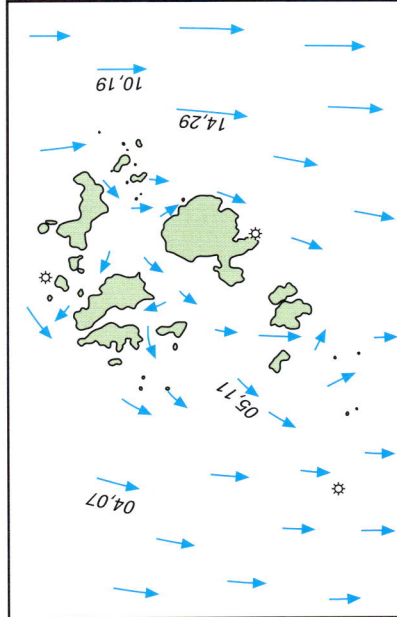

0400 AFTER
HW DEVONPORT
0455 AFTER
HW ST MARY'S

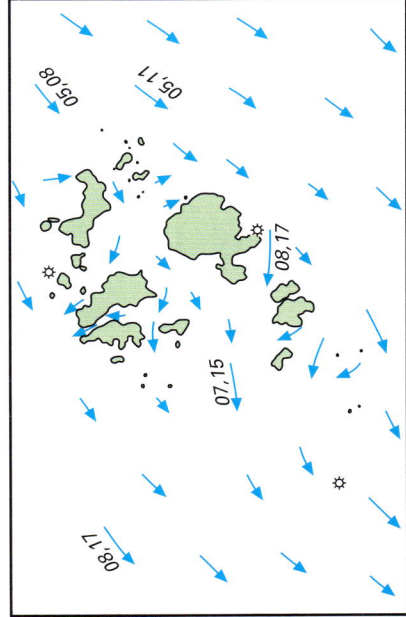

Tidal streams (see pages 8-9)

The inshore tidal streams tend to follow the line of the coast, flowing into bays and out at the far end, while offshore streams follow a straighter line up or down channel. When clearing most bays and channels, one must allow for considerable set both into and out of them. In Scilly there are overfalls and tidal eddies which must be allowed for off many points and headlands, while note should be taken that heights, times, speeds and directions of tidal streams around the islands are most irregular. These factors are also affected by the presence of high or low pressure so, even with sophisticated electronic equipment, the best way to cope with the vagaries of tidal streams and currents is to adjust your vessel's course and speed by visual assessment of progress.

To N, W and S of the islands the weakest and strongest streams generally run as follows:

Local HW	Devonport HW	Dover HW	Direction	Rate (knots) Springs	Neaps
+0540	−0550	+0015	NW	¾	¼
−0345	−0250	+0315	NE–ENE	1½	¾
−0245	−0150	+0415			
−0045	+0010	+0615	SE	¾	½
+0215	+0310	−0310	SW	1½	¾
+0315	+0410	−0210			

To E of the islands and between them and the mainland coast the weakest and strongest streams are:

Local HW	Devonport HW	Dover HW	Direction	Rate (knots) Springs	Neaps
−0245	−0150	+0415	ENE	1	½
+0015	+0110	−0510	SSE	2	1
+0415	+0510	−0110	WNW	1	½
−0405	−0310	+0255	N	1¼	¾

Note Tidal streams in the various sounds and anchorages are given in the pilotage directions for the particular area.

Tidal heights

Mean tidal heights are given below.

Local HW is Devonport −0055, Dover +0605

MHWS	MHWN	ML	MLWS	MLWN
5·7m	4·3m	3·2m	0·7m	2·0m

Chart datum is LAT which is 2·91m below ordnance datum.

High water at Scilly

For mariners who keep track of the phases of the moon, High Water Full and Change is at about 1700 hours. High Water Springs is at 0600 and 1800 hours. All times UT.

Radio

There are a large number of radio navigational aids and services in the area of the Isles of Scilly. In particular, VHF Ch 64 is recommended for weather information, navigational warnings and traffic lists to vessels in Scilly.

Racons

The approaches to the Isles of Scilly are endowed with three useful Racons:

Location	Identification	Range
Bishop Rock Lt	T	18M
Seven Stones LtF	O	15M
Wolf Rock Lt	T	10M

Radio navigational aids and DGPS

Before embarking on a visit to Scilly, yachtsmen are advised to study the *Admiralty List of Radio Signals Vol 2*. With the introduction of a Differential Global Positioning System service, many Marine RDF stations are being phased out, although certain strategically placed stations are being retained and are being incorporated into the new system. It appears that aero RDF stations are unaffected by the changes. It is also the case that, in the UK, corrections transmitted by beacons in the DGPS service can only be decoded with the aid of specialised equipment on board the receiving vessel. Within the area of Scilly the only former marine RDF beacon (now transmitting DGPS corrections as from 6 April 1998) is Lizard light (284kHz 100M). French marine RDF beacons which still offer a direction-finding facility for old RDF sets are listed below.

Marine radiobeacons

Roches Douvres 308kHz *RD* (·—·/—···) 70M
Ile Vierge 314kHz *VG* (···—/——·) 70M
Ile d'Ouessant 301kHz *CA* (—·—·/·—) 100M

Note All are continuous.

Air radiobeacons

Penzance 333kHz *PH* (·——·/····) 15M 50°07'·67N 5°31'W Sunrise to sunset
St Mary's, Isles of Scilly 321kHz *STM* (···/—/——) 15M 49°54'·82N 6°17'·43W Sunrise to sunset

Coast radio stations

Land's End (GLD)

RT Transmits 2182, 2670, **2782**, **3610**kHz
Receives 2111, 2120, 2182kHz Continuous
Traffic lists 2670kHz at 0233, 0303, 0633, 0733, 0903, 1033, 1433, 1503, 1833, 1933, 2103, 2233
VHF Transmits and Receives on Ch 16, **27, 64** Continuous
Traffic lists Ch 27, 64 at 0233, 0303, 0633, 0733, 0903, 1033, 1433, 1503, 1833, 1933, 2103, 2233
VHF Direction finding station operates from St Mary's, Isles of Scilly

Radio weather services

Below are listed alternative sources of weather data.
BBC Radio 4. Times are local
Radio 4 198kHz (1515m) and FM 92·4–94·6MHz broadcasts weather services in accordance with the following schedule:

Warnings of gales are broadcast at the end of news bulletins or at the first change of programme following receipt.

⋆ Denotes forecasts of particular interest to mariners.

Tx slot (6.4.98)	Title	Duration	Content	Days
0014	Weather	1'	3-day	Sun night
0029	Weather	1'	3-day	Mon– Fri night
0022	Weather	3'	Detailed inc 3-day	Sat night
⋆0048	Ships 1. General synopsis 2. Area forecast 3. Coastal stations 4. Inshore waters	11'	Detailed	Every day
⋆0535	Ships 1. General synopsis 2. Area forecast 3. Coastal stations 4. Inshore waters	7'	Detailed	Every day
⋆0542	Weather	3'	Long-range (of particular interest to sailors)	Sun
0556	Weather	3'	Topical (Leisure forecast)	Sat
0556	Weather	3'	Detailed (UK and World forecast)	Sun
0604	Weather	1'	General	Sat only
0657	Weather	2'	Detailed	Every day
0730	Weather	10"	Synopsis	Mon–Sat
0757	Weather	2'	Detailed	Every day
0830	Weather	10"	Synopsis	
⋆1201	Ships (LW only)	3'	Detailed	Every day
1204	1. General synopsis 2. Area forecast			
1257–	Weather	2'	Detailed	Every day
⋆1754	Ships (LW only) 1. General synopsis 2. Area forecast	3'	Detailed	Mon–Fri
⋆1754	Ships 1. General synopsis 2. Area forecast	3'	Detailed	Sat & Sun
1757	Weather	2'	Detailed	Every day
2208	Weather	30"	General	Every day

Start Point VHF Ch 26. Storm warnings at end of first silence period after receipt and at 0303, 0903, 1503 and 2103. Weather messages on request and at 0733 and 1933.

Land's End (GLD) MF 2670kHz (speech) 0·5kW. Storm warnings at end of first silence period after receipt and at 0303, 0903, 1503, 2103. Weather messages on request and at 0733 and 1933. **VHF** Ch 27, 64 0·025kW. Storm warnings at end of first silence period and at 0303, 0903, 1503, 2103. Weather messages as above.

Radio France LF[1,2] France Inter 162kHz (French) 2000kW. Weather messages at Sat, Sun; 0654, 2003 local time. **MF**[1,2] Rennes 711kHz (French) 300kW. Brest 1404kHz. A3E (French) 20kW. Weather messages 0655 local time.

1. Times are UT except where otherwise stated.
2. Broadcast given 1 hour earlier when British summer time (BST) is in force.

Local radio

The following local radio stations give coastal weather forecasts and small craft warnings as follows:

Local time, Mon–Fri at 0725, 0825, 1225 Sat at 0725, 0825, 1325 Sun at 0825, 0925

Mid and West 103·9 FM and 630kHz
North and East 95·2 FM and 657kHz
Isles of Scilly 96·0 FM

Radio navigational warnings. Times are UT

Start Point VHF Ch 26. Navigational warnings at 0233, 0633, 1033, 1433, 1833, 2233. Decca warnings for SW British Chain and Irish Chain.

Land's End GLD MF 2670kHz. 0·5kW. VHF Ch 27, 64. Navigational warnings at 0233, 0633, 1033, 1433, 1833, 2233. Decca warnings for SW British Chain and Irish Chain.

BBC Radio 4 Messages of unusual importance or urgency.

Port radio

Harbour Call	VHF Ch	Hours manned	☎
Falmouth Hbr Radio	16, 11, 12	0800–1700	01326 312285/ 314379 Fax 211352
Penzance	16, 09, 12	0830–1630	01736 66113 and (outside office hours) 61119

Harbourmaster and Pilots

Newlyn[2] Harbourmaster	16, 09, 12	0800–1700	01736 62523
St Mary's[3] Harbourmaster	16, 14	0800–1700	01720 422768
Padstow	16	0830–1630	01841 532239

Also manned on Saturdays:
1. Sat 0800–1230
2. Sat 0800–1200
3. Sat 0800–1200 (winter only)

Note Times are UT and need adjustment during summer months.

Telephone weather service

Local weather forecasts and shipping data ☎ (0891) 500 458

NAVTEX

Transmissions of weather information covering the four sea areas adjacent to Scilly (Fastnet, Lundy, Sole and Plymouth) are available at 0818 and 2018 UTC from Niton (Isle of Wight).

Weather information via Internet and fax

The UK Met Office offers services on their web site http://www.met-office.gov.uk
or via e-mail: metweb@meto.gov.uk
Fax services are also offered.
For free information ☎ 0374 555 888.
Also available on ☎ 01344 854 435.
From abroad ☎ +44 374 555 888.

Navigational aids and safety

Major lights and fog signals at or near Scilly

Bishop Rock Fl(2)15s44m24M Horn Mo(N)90s Racon Heli-platform. Grey round granite tower. Partially obscured 204°-211°, obscured 211°-233°, 236°-259°

St Mary's 2 rows F.R lights on TV mast 119m near Telegraph Tower. F.R lights on radio mast on control tower at airport and mast S of airfield

Peninnis Head Fl.20s36m17M White round metal tower on black metal framework tower, black cupola 231°-vis-117°, part obscured 048°-083° within 5M

Round Island N side Fl.10s55m24M. Horn(4)60s White round tower 021°-vis-288° Continuous

Round I. lighthouse, looking N from St Helen's

Lizard E tower Fl.3s70m26M Horn 30s White 8-sided tower at E end of building 120°-vis-250° Storm sigs. A continuous light of low power may sometimes be seen within 12M

Tater-du Fl(3)15s34m23M Horn(2)30s White round tower 241°-vis-074° F.R.31m13M 060°-vis-074° over Runnel Stone and in places 074°-077° within 4M

Wolf Rock Fl.15s34m23M Horn 30s Racon Grey round granite tower, black lantern Heli-platform Continuous

Longships Iso.WR.10s35m18/15M Horn 10s Grey round granite tower on highest rock 189°-R-208°-R(unintens)-307°-R-327°-W-189° Helicopter platform Continuous. F.R on radio mast 4·9M NE

Pendeen Fl(4)15s59m16M Horn 20s White round tower and dwellings 042°-vis-240°

Bishop Rock lighthouse, looking E

Wolf Rock lighthouse, looking NE

Crow Rock
    beacon   Hulman beacon

Hulman beacon, marking the starboard side of the approach channel from St Mary's Road to New Grimsby; looking roughly E

Seven Stones LtF Fl(3)30s12m25M Horn(3)60s Racon. Red hull, light-tower amidships. Continuous

Beacons in Scilly
St Martin's Daymark tower (56m) red and white bands on E end of island
St Mary's Pool Ldg beacons 097° *Front* White triangle on a pyramid base. *Rear* Black St Andrew's Cross on a pole. Both beacons have a fixed red light at night
St Agnes old LtHo White tower in centre of island
Crow Rock beacon, Crow Sound Isolated danger beacon (11m). Black, red, black, topmark, stands on a rock (dries 4·6m)
Woolpack Point, St Mary's Sound S card, yellow over black with topmark
Hulman beacon S entrance to New Grimsby Sound. Triangular green radar reflector on pole (and see page 14)
Little Rag Ledge beacon 300m to NNW of above, square red radar reflector on pole

The beacon at Little Rag Ledge, marking the port side of the same channel; looking W

Buoyage
The buoyage on this section of coast is the IALA maritime buoyage system 'A' as shown in the table below. Both the lateral and cardinal systems are in use. All buoys listed below have radar reflectors.

Coastguard Services in the SW area of Britain
All coastguard services are co-ordinated by Falmouth Maritime Rescue Co-ordination Centre which maintains a continuous watch on distress, calling and safety VHF channel 16. The working channel is 67. Other available frequencies are VHF channels 06, 10, 73 and MF, also HF. Digital Selective Calling. Distress and Safety Ch 70

continuous. The area is covered by five separate aerials spaced out along the coast.

Customs offices
Customs and excise offices are located as follows: Penzance Custom House ☎ 01736 63366; Isles of Scilly Custom House, St Mary's ☎ 01720 422571.

Visitors arriving from non-EU countries must clear customs on arrival.

Lifeboats
Lifeboats are stationed as follows: Cadgwith (Lizard); Penlee; St Ives; Sennen Cove; St Mary's (Isles of Scilly).

Hazards and restrictions
Overfalls
There are some overfalls around the islands and there are many smaller overfalls in the sounds and channels which appear when the local current is opposed to a strong wind.

Fishing hazards
A lot of fishing takes place along this part of the coast and a careful watch is necessary in order to avoid fishing boats and their gear which may stretch in any direction. The following types of fishing may be met with:

Trawling Boats of up to 30m are used for trawling and dredging for fish and scallops. They are hampered by their gear and must be given a good berth. Sometimes they work in pairs with gear between.

Drifting Boats of up to 13m are used, usually at night, in drifting for herring, mackerel and pilchard. They operate with trains of nets extending up to 2M supported on the surface by small floats, the end being marked by a lighted can buoy. The vessels usually have a small mizzen sail and should be passed to leeward.

Long lining Lines which can extend up to 7M are laid along the sea bed and are marked by lighted can buoys at intervals. The small boats which lay the lines usually stay in position with their gear.

Trolling In the spring, summer and autumn, fleets of small boats will be seen trolling for mackerel with hand lines which extend only some 10m behind the boat. A few of the boats will be stationary, 'jigging' for mackerel. The area where this fishing is taking place should be avoided if possible.

Seining A fishing vessel encircles a shoal of fish with a purse-shaped net supported by floats. When

Buoys

Name	Location	Type	Topmark	Colour	Remarks
Hats	Crow Sound	Card S		Y over B	Off S edge shoal (cover 0·4m)
Old Wreck	N of Annet	Card N		B over Y	Rock (covers 1m) 150m to S
Gunner	Broad Sound	Card S		Y over B	Awash rock 300m to N
Round Rock	Broad Sound	Card N		B over Y	Rock (dries 2·4m) 300m to S
Bartholomew Ledges	St Mary's Sound	Can light	■	R	Fl.R.5s Rock (covers 0·6m) 50m SW
Spanish Ledge	St Mary's Sound	Card E		BYB	Rocks awash and covered 200m to W

the circle has been completed the ends of the net are joined and drawn in. Nets may be 400m long and at a depth of 75m or more.

Pelagic fishing Midwinter single and pair trawling and seining September to March. Up to 50 vessels may be encountered in a small area.

Potting and tangle netting Fleets (lines) of pots are set on the sea bottom to catch shellfish. The pots can be set singly, but are usually in lines ½M long, marked by can or other types of buoy, which must be avoided as the gear is very heavy and will damage propellers, etc.

Diving Professional and amateur divers operate in the islands, usually near rocks or wrecks. The parent boat should be in the immediate vicinity of the divers. This flies the International Code flag 'A' (white and blue vertical halves, swallow tail). The area should be given a wide berth and a sharp lookout kept for any divers surfacing up to 1M away.

Experimental area
An experimental area 1M square exists 1M to NW of Shipman Head, Bryher. Anchoring and fishing are prohibited. See plan page 26.

Historic wrecks
There are many wreck sites around the islands. Two are designated historic wreck sites: one is at Tearing Ledge and the other at Bartholomew Ledges (see plan pages 38-9). Anchoring, fishing and diving are forbidden near these areas; seek local advice.

Underwater cables
There are many underwater power and telephone cables which have been laid between individual islands and also to the mainland. Where these cables come ashore, there are beacons with yellow ♦ topmarks (see plans for details). The sea is usually so clear that cables may be visible on the sea bed. However, it is strongly recommended that anchors are buoyed so that a trip line is available to recover the anchor if necessary.

Exercise area
See page 18.

Traffic Separation Schemes
See page 18.

Restricted landings
To protect wildlife and limit disturbance of birds, landing is not allowed on specific islands between 15 March and 20 August without a written permit from the Isles of Scilly Environmental Trust, St Mary's. The islands are: Western Rocks, Melledgan, Annet, Norrard Rocks, Green Island (off Samson), Stony Island, Men-a-vaur and Tean.

Isles of Scilly Marine Park
This park has been established by the Duchy of Cornwall, the Isles of Scilly Environmental Trust, the Sea Fisheries Committee, the council of the Isles of Scilly and English Heritage.

It is concerned with the area enclosed by the 50m contour to the height of HAT, and the marine plants and animals therein. A useful brochure is available from the tourist information centre at Hugh Town, and should be acquired and studied by anyone wishing to explore the area both above and below the water level.

Charts
Admiralty *34, 883, 1148*
French *6745, 7108*
Imray *C7, C10, C18*

Magnetic variation
5°45'W (1999) decreasing by 08' each year.

New navigation marks in the approach to St Mary's
At the time of going to press, the St Mary's harbourmaster reported that a complete review of navigational aids in Scilly is being conducted with representatives of Trinity House. The following alterations have either been put into effect or are planned:

1. Hulman beacon. An all-round solar-powered light, Fl.G.6s1·5M, has recently been installed on this beacon which lies in the seaway between St Mary's Road and Tresco Flats.
2. A port hand light buoy, Fl.R (no details available) is intended for installation during 1999 on Bacon Ledge, which lies about 350m NW of the quayhead light at St Mary's Pool.
3. During 1999 it is intended to change the characteristics of the day marks and lights of the beacons which lead into St Mary's Pool on a bearing of 097°. The triangle on the forward beacon and the St Andrew's cross on the rear beacon are to be painted yellow with vertical black stripes. It is hoped this will aid recognition of these leading marks among the forest of yacht masts. The lights on these leading beacons – at present F.R – are to be changed as follows: the forward beacon to carry an Oc.R over an Oc. The rear beacon to carry an Oc over an Oc.R. It is hoped that the new lights will eliminate any possibility of confusion with red lights situated further inshore.
4. 'In the near future' it is hoped to install an isolated danger mark on The Cow, which lies about 525m N of the quayhead light at St Mary's Pool.

II. Approaches to Scilly

1. Outer approaches

Yachtsmen arriving from the N or NW should not have to worry about the Seven Stones rocks which lie well to the E of the approach track. Details of these rocks are shown below and they should be given a wide berth. As a vessel closes the land from the N it should be possible to recognise Round Island lighthouse, white (Fl.10s55m24M) and the St Martin's daymark (see photos pages 12 and 5).

The distant approach from the W has no hazards, but it is suggested that those arriving from this direction, especially for the first time or in less than perfect visibility, should opt for close approach from N or S. The western aspect of Scilly has only one impeccable navigational mark and that is the great lighthouse called Bishop Rock (Fl(2)15s44m24M Racon). Otherwise the rocky outcrops are daunting, dangerous and largely unrecognisable. The Broad Sound which leads into Scilly NE of Bishop Rock is anything but broad and although there are three buoys in this approach, they are by no means obvious in poor visibility; if a yacht strays from the narrow paths of entrance, disaster very soon threatens by way of hidden rocks. These dangerous waters, together with the Atlantic swell, are met three or four miles offshore. In addition, tidal streams can run strongly and eddies are unpredictable. Visibility has only to shut down a little to make navigational fixes difficult to obtain. The important anchorages are easier to reach from directions other than W, and, generally speaking, with more safety.

There are no offshore dangers in the southern approach. The conspicuous lighthouse on Bishop Rock should be seen from afar. In the closer approach the old lighthouse on St Agnes will be seen (see photo page 4).

The passage from the E (the mainland) requires careful calculation of the time of departure so as to arrive in Scilly with enough time to go to anchor in daylight. One should leave anchorage off Penzance or Newlyn at first light if possible and a departure from Land's End at around half ebb (HW Dover −3 hours) towards a point S of Scilly should maximise the use of the tide.

With a fair wind at the start of the westbound stream, an early morning departure from, say, Helford River, also makes it possible for most cruising yachts to arrive at Scilly in daylight.

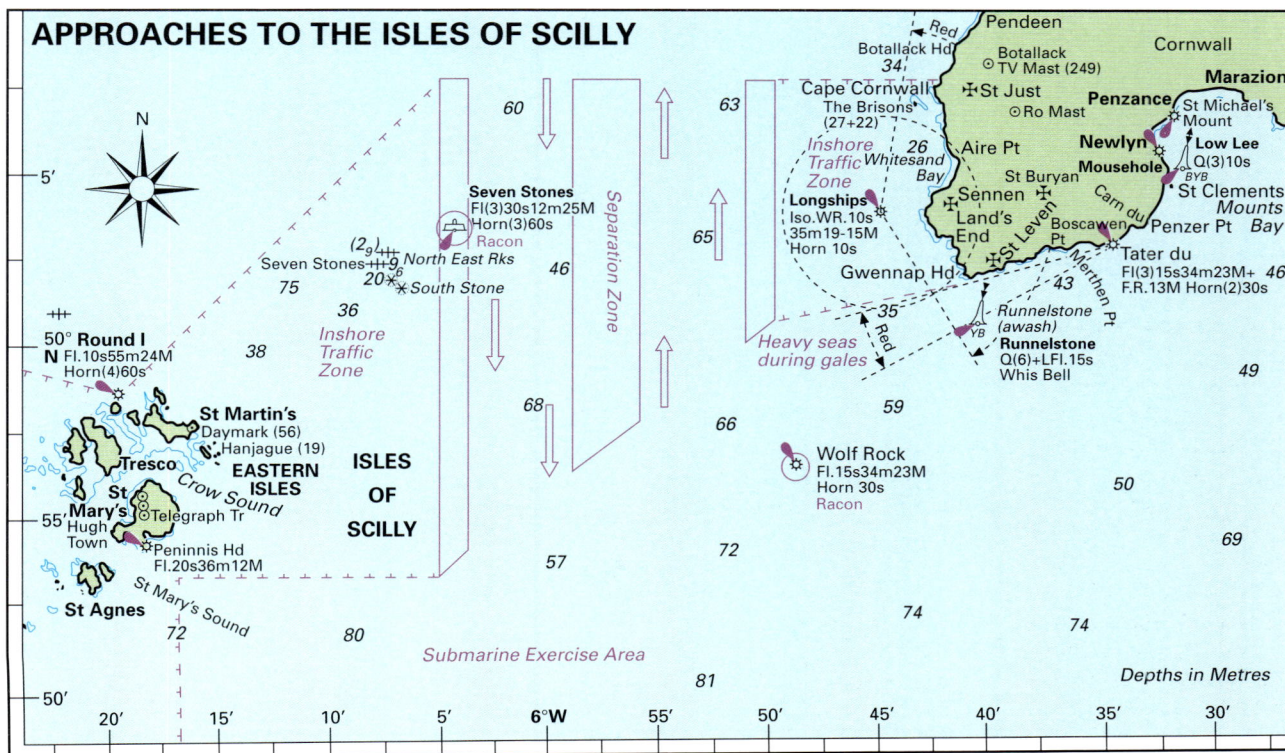

APPROACHES TO THE ISLES OF SCILLY

THE ISLES OF SCILLY LEADING LINES

This plan should not be used for navigation

Line AZ South end of St Agnes in line with Bishop Rk Lt (261°).

Line A Pidney Brow (S St Agnes) on The Hoe (241°) clears Gilstone (St Mary's) (dries 4m).

Line B Haycocks (N Annet) clear S of Peninnis Head (267°) clears Gilstone (St Mary's) (dries 4m).

Line C N Carn of Mincarlo on SW edge of Great Minalto (307°).

Line D Steval on Telegraph Tower (045°). Alter course to N.

Line F Samson Hill (Bryher) on NE edge Innisidgen (N St Mary's) (284°) leads up centre of entrance.

Line G Centre of Men-a-Vaur in line with St Helen's landing Carn 322° entry/exit SE to/from St Helen's Pool.

Line H Hats buoy on Green Island (Tresco) (4m) (289°) leads to entrance to Crow Sound.

Line I S end of Samson on Nut Rock and Crow Rock beacon (250°) clears Queen's Ledge.

Line J St Agnes old lighthouse on Steval (207°) leads towards St Mary's Harbour from Crow Sound.

Line K1 TV Tower just open Goat's Point on 180°20' leads E of Black Rock or line

Line K2 Bab's Carn on Pednbean on 154° leads W of Black Rock

Line L Guther's Island on 158° with Toll's Island open to E and Innisidgen open W.

Line M Green Island (Tresco) on 216°.

Line N Star Castle Hotel (St Mary's) in line with E Gap Rock (2·3m) on 182°.

Line O Hangman I. in line with Steval 344° leads between Round Rock (Gugh) and Spanish Ledges.

Line P Hedge Rock (14m) on Southward Carn (St Martin's) on 074°.

Line Q Rock 3·8m high between Merchant's Point and SW side Northwethel leads through the entrance to Old Grimsby Sound on 124°.

Line R Island Hotel on Long Point slip leads away SE from Old Grimsby Harbour clear of Blockhouse Point on 292° (stern transit).

Experimental Area

Old Grimsby Sound

New Grimsby Sound

T

O

Shipman Head (24)

Gimble Pt

BRYHER

Beacon Hill (42)

Northern (Norrard) Rocks

Scilly Rk (19)

Hangman I.

(Bn)⊙ 43

Queen's Ledge

Gweal (29)

Merrick I.

Maiden Bower (18)

Black Rks (2)

Castle Bryher (23)

Samson Hill 40

Tresco Flats

Seal Rk (9)

Illiswilgig (11)

Buzza Rk

SAMSON

North Carn Mincarlo (16)

Bream Ledge

Southward Well Pt

North Channel

Great Minalto (7)

(6)

V

Y

AA

Old Wreck

BY

Great Smith (8)

49° 54' N

Crim Rks

(3₂)

Gunners Ledge

W

Ruddy

Haycocks (18)

The Cow

(2)

Gunner

YB

Shark's Fin

Minmanueth (13)

16

Burnt Island

19

Old LtHo

Carn Irish

Broad Sound

X

Round Rk

BY

ANNET

Menrounds

Z

ST AGNES

Isinvrank (4)

Lethegus Rks

13

Muncoy Neck

Brothers

Gt Crebawethan (6)

WESTERN ROCKS

Smith Sound

Lt Crebawethan (5)

Grebawethan Neck

Melledgan (7)

Bishop Rock
Fl(2)15s44m24M
Horn Mo(N)90s

Retarrier Ledges

Biggal (4₈)

Gorregan Neck

Rosevear (11)

Rags

Gorregan (15)

Crebinicks (5₂)

(3)

Rosevean (14)

Gilstone Ledges

EASTERN ISLES

N

Depth in Metres

0   1

Nautical Miles

Round I
Fl.10s55m24M
Horn(4)60s

K2
N
K1

Lion Rk (8)

Pernagie

White I (26)

St Helen's Gap

St
Helen's
(35)

Great Merrick Ledge

St Martin's Bay

St Martin's Head

Pednbrose (12)

Daymark (56)
RW

E Gap Rk
St Helen's Pool

Goats Pt
Bns

ST MARTIN'S

Higher Town

Hanjague (19)

Northwethel

Tean
Old Man

St Martin's Flats

Mouls (2)

Old Grimsby Beacon Hill (42)

P
Long Pt
Foreman's I
Hedge (8) Rk

L

Cruthers Pt

32

Great Ganilly

Great Innisvouls (23)

Blockhouse Pt
Bns
R

Lt Cheese Rk

Gt Cheese Rk
Tea Ledge

M

Little Ganilly

Great Arthur

New Grimsby

TRESCO

Bn

W Craggyellis

Guther's I

Gt Ganinick

Biggal (1)

Appletree Pt
Bn

Green I

Crow Bar

Lt Ganinick

Ridge Higher Corner

4 6 Trinity Rk

Carn Near
Crow Pt
Hulman Rk

Crow Rk
Bn

Bar Pt

Hats
Hats

H

I

Bant's Carn

Bn
39

Innisdgen (7)

F

Nut Rk

J
Creeb

TV Mast (119)
Ro Masts
Telegraph Tr (63)
Ro Mast

Toll's I (13)

Crow Sound

Carn Morval Pt
Bn

ST MARY'S

U

D

St Mary's Road

Rat I
F.R
F.R

Gap Pt

Port Hellick

A

BB

HUGH TOWN
Old Town

Airport

Woodcock Ledge

Steval

Star Castle Hotel

Newfoundland Pt

Woolpack Pt

Porth Cressa

Tolman's Pt

B

Fl.R 5s
Bn

Peninnis Head
Fl.20s36m12M

Gilstone (4)

AZ

Kittern (17)
The Bow
Bell
BYB

Spanish Ledges

St Mary's Sound

holomew edges

GUGH

The Cove

Hoe Pt

31

C

O

Pidney Brow

Great Wingletang

Line S	Crow Rock beacon on TV Tower (160°) leads towards St Mary's Road.
Line T	W side Hangman Island on Star Castle Hotel on St Mary's on 157° leads into New Grimsby Sound.
Line U	Merrick Island on Hangman Island on 340° (stern transit) leads over Tresco Flats.
Line V	St Agnes old lighthouse between the two summits of Great Smith on 130° leads through North Channel.
Line W	N summit of Great Ganilly just open of N of Bant's Carn on 059° leads into St Mary's Road.
Line X	Star Castle Hotel in line with the N Haycock leads into Broad Sound entrance on 067°. Do not mistake the Ruddy (dries 4·3m, and lies 200m to WNW of the N Haycock) for the N Haycock itself.
Line Y	Castle Bryher between the summits of Great Smith on 351° leads up Smith Sound.
Line Z	Old lighthouse on St Agnes on Penny Ledges on 091°.
Line AA	Carn Irish open N of Great Smith clears Halftide Ledges and Bristolman rock on 234° (stern transit).
BB	St Martin's Daymark on summit of Creeb on 041° clears Woodcock Ledge.

20' 19' 18' 17' 16' 15' 14' 13' 12'

17

A night passage with arrival before daylight is also practical from points of departure on mainland Britain, and this timing of arrival is very worthwhile when coming across the English Channel from the S or SE (see page 34)

Arrival at Scilly with the sun behind you but with the advantage of having fixed your position before dawn with the help of the various navigational lights has much to recommend it, provided visibility is good. Subsequent observation of the daymarks on St Martin and St Agnes together with Bishop Rock lighthouse will much assist entry. Yachtsmen approaching Scilly with this light on a bearing of 261° (line AZ) before and after dawn are in a good position to make a satisfactory landfall in southern Scilly.

When on passage from mainland anchorages off Newlyn and Penzance, the Runnel Stone, yellow and black south cardinal bell and whistle buoy (Q(6)+LFl.15s) with ⌄ topmark, must be left to starboard and a wide berth should be given to the Longships rocks which lie due W of Land's End about one mile offshore. The Longships lighthouse (Iso.WR.10s35m19/15M) stands on the tallest rock, and consists of a grey granite tower with a helicopter landing pad.

When on passage westward from the Lizard, Wolf Rock lies almost directly on the course to Scilly. It has a lighthouse (Fl.15s34m23M Racon) consisting of a grey round granite tower with black lantern and a helicopter landing pad. It is built on a rock (dries 3·4m) which is steep-to. This lighthouse is very useful for navigating the passage, but one should avoid the heavy overfalls which occur in bad weather to the W of the rock with wind against tide.

A Traffic Separation Scheme (TSS) lies N/S between Land's End and the Seven Stones and a red light float with a light tower (Fl(3)30s12m25M Racon) guards the western edge of the TSS about two miles NE of the Seven Stones. This area of rocks is the only such hazard in the outer approaches to Scilly and should be given a wide berth. Do not pass between the light float and the rocks.

Traffic Separation Schemes also exist to the S and W of the Isles of Scilly. These schemes require traversing yachts to present the whole of their length at 90° to traffic using the separation scheme. Whatever the wind and tide are doing, yachts must maintain a right-angled appearance so there is no doubt of their intention to cross the TSS by the shortest distance, even if, in so doing, the vessel makes good a diagonal course. If under sail in light

winds, an engine, if available, should be used to speed the crossing. A plan of the Traffic Separation Schemes E of Scilly is shown on page 15.

The other feature of the outer approaches to Scilly is an exercise area used by British and French submarines and surface vessels between 47°30'N and 50°30'N and to the east of 10°W.

Sea ferry and helicopter services operate between Penzance and the islands; there are also fixed-wing aircraft from Land's End and, in the holiday season, from Exeter, Plymouth and Newquay. Usually the aircraft follow the most direct route and offer a rough check on navigation.

2. Close approaches

Approach from the east

Directions

Leading marks
Approach from E
Line AZ S end of St Agnes in line Bishop Rock light on 261°. The easiest approach to St Mary's Sound
Approach from NE
Line A Pidney Brow (S St Agnes) on The Hoe (241°) clears Gilstone (St Mary's) (dries 4m)
Approach from E
Line B Haycocks (N Annet) clear S of Peninnis Head (267°) clears Gilstone (St Mary's) (dries 4m)
Through St Mary's Sound
Line C N Carn of Mincarlo on SW edge of Great Minalto (307°)
End of St Mary's Sound
Line BB St Martin's Daymark on summit of Creeb 041° clears Woodcock Ledge
Line D Steval on Telegraph Tower (045°). Course may be altered to N

The easiest entry to Scilly from the E (and S) is probably via St Mary's Sound, which separates St Mary's from Gugh and St Agnes to the SW. In SW-W-NW winds and swell there may be heavy seas over the shoals at the NW end of the passage and with a strong E-SE wind against tide the passage can be rough and unpleasant. Good visibility is necessary to see the leading marks, but the channel is buoyed and can be used, with care, in poor visibility. There is a minimum depth of 10m and minimum width of 300m on this approach.

Yachtsmen approaching from the E can take advantage of the tall, 44m-high Bishop Rock light, the structure of which can be seen from many miles

Tidal streams
Stream begins in St Mary's Sound:

Local HW	Devonport HW	Dover HW	Direction	Max rate (knots) Springs	Neaps	Remarks
−0450	−0545	+0115	SE	1¾	¾	Generally in
+0140	+0045	−0440	NW	1¾	¾	direction of sound

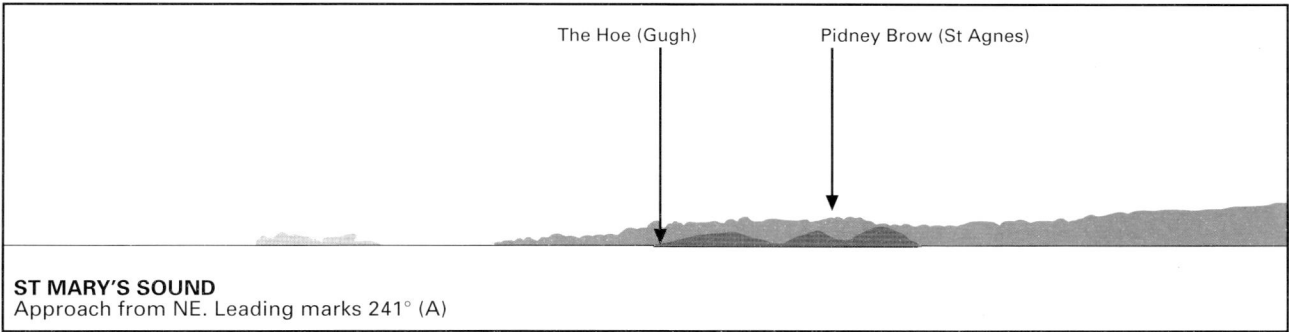

ST MARY'S SOUND
Approach from NE. Leading marks 241° (A)

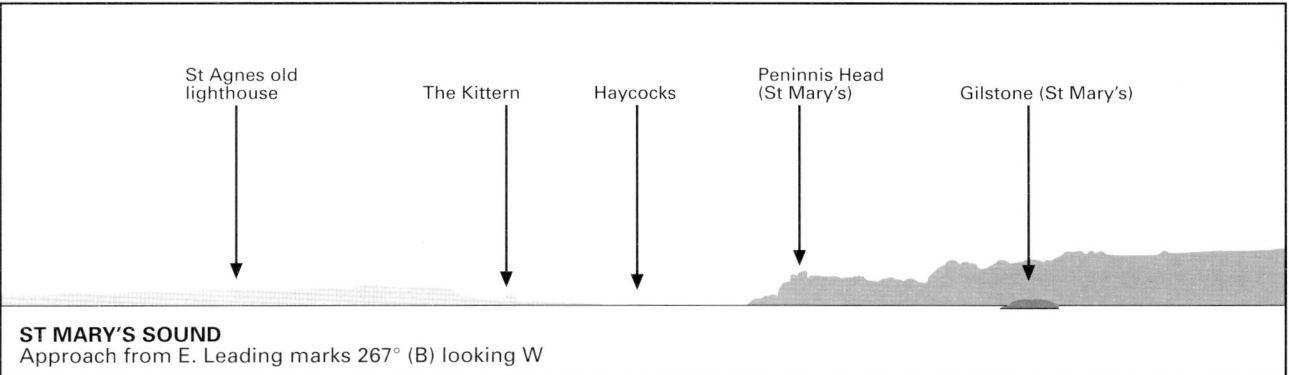

ST MARY'S SOUND
Approach from E. Leading marks 267° (B) looking W

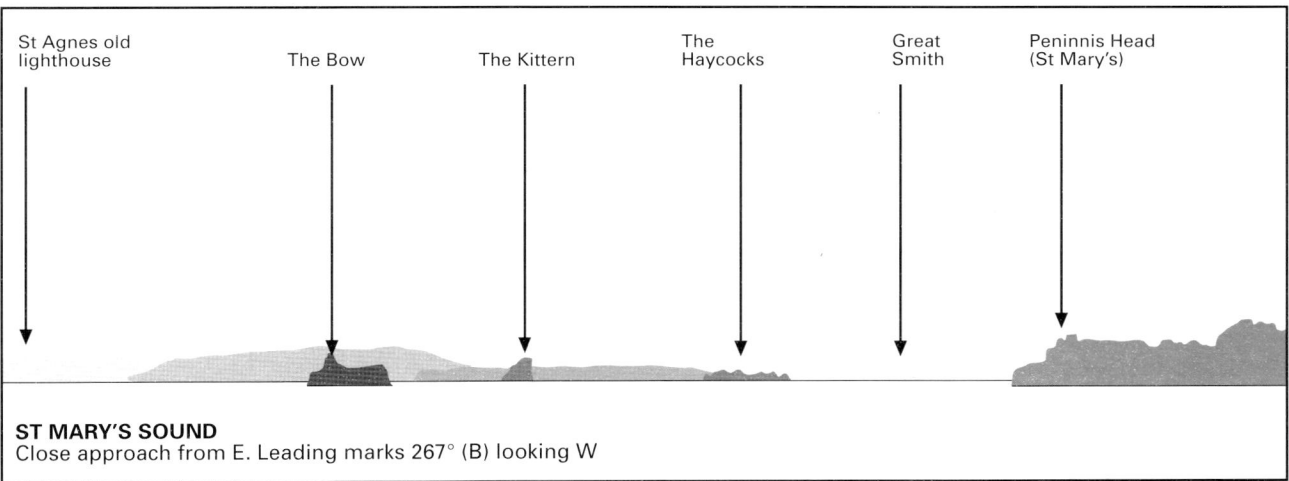

ST MARY'S SOUND
Close approach from E. Leading marks 267° (B) looking W

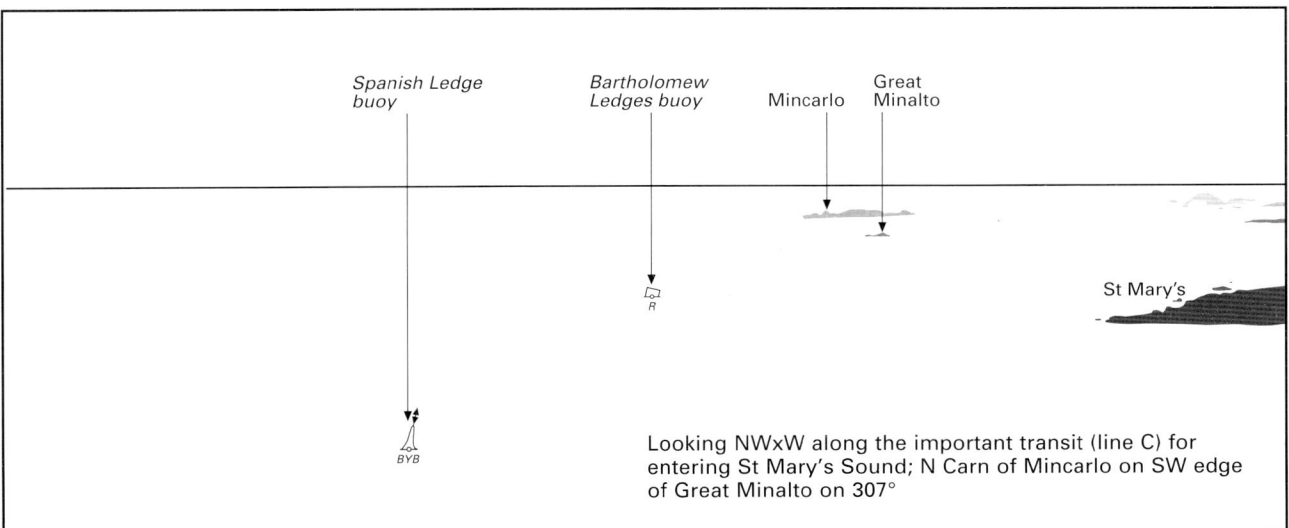

Looking NWxW along the important transit (line C) for
entering St Mary's Sound; N Carn of Mincarlo on SW edge
of Great Minalto on 307°

to the E of Scilly. If proceeding to any of the three most useful southern anchorages, which are The Cove, Porth Cressa and St Mary's Pool (on St Mary's), one should keep Bishop Rock light on a bearing of 261° (line AZ). This gives the S coast of St Mary's a wide berth and clears all obstacles on the distant and middle approach. The bearing also transits the southern point of St Agnes and makes an excellent line of approach to The Cove between St Agnes and Gugh.

The Cove

About a mile off the S coast of St Agnes, the bay known as The Cove will open up to starboard. A yacht may enter when the prominent rock called The Cow is sighted in the middle of the bar, bearing approximately NNW. Keep The Cow in the middle of the bar and proceed straight in to find anchorage toward the head of The Cove.

Porth Cressa

Yachtsmen using the same transit and bearing on Bishop Rock light (line AZ) and wishing to enter Porth Cressa will find themselves on the charted transit 'North Carn of Mincarlo in line with western extremity of Great Minalto 307°' (line C), when Peninnis Head lighthouse bears approximately 335° distant about one mile (see diagram page 19). Unfortunately, the N carn of Mincarlo is much bigger than the tiny rock of Great Minalto which can cause confusion. If in doubt about the transit, one should pick out the Spanish Ledge buoy which lies close to port of the transit line. Spanish Ledge is an E cardinal bell buoy, black and yellow with a black ♦ topmark, marking a group of covered rocks one of which is awash at LAT. When the buoy lies close abeam to port, alter course due N and enter Porth Cressa leaving Biggal (2·4m) about 150m abeam to port. Stand on for a further 100m until The Wras (3·4m) lies abeam to port and then enter the anchorage on a course of about N x W.

St Agnes   The Bar   The Cow   Gugh

The Cove, between St Agnes and Gugh, looking roughly NNW from the entrance

Wras Biggal   Raveen

Spanish Ledge buoy

Porth Cressa (St Mary's) at HW, looking NxW into the harbour

St Mary's Pool

If proceeding to St Mary's Pool, follow the Mincarlo/Minalto transit on 307° (line C) past Woolpack Point to starboard, where there is a S cardinal beacon, yellow over black with a ⍖ (7m) standing close to a rock which dries 0·6m, and then leave the red can buoy called Bartholomew Ledges close abeam to port. This buoy is a red can light buoy (Fl.R.5s) marking some rocks that cover 0·6m. Continue on this course until the daymark on St Martin's is sighted on a bearing of 041° which is in transit with Creeb (line BB) – the westernmost rock on the NW coast of St Mary's. Follow this course for about ¾ mile to clear Woodcock Ledge to the SE. This leads to the first of three possible approaches to St Mary's harbour:

Approach 1

From west between Bacon Ledge (to the N) and Rat Island (to the S). This is the best entrance for those arriving for the first time. It is marked by two beacons in line 097°. The St Mary's lifeboat is

Beacons in line

The leading marks for entering St Mary's Pool from the W on 097° (approach 1)

Buzza Hill tower

White mark on shelter

Scillonian

Buzza Hill tower

White mark on shelter

The leading marks for approaching St Mary's Pool from the NW on 151° (approach 2)

almost directly on this approach when she is secured on station and the two day marks are in line behind. The lower front mark consists of a white triangle on a pole, while the higher mark behind is a black St Andrew's cross on a pole. Each mark now shows a fixed red light at night.

Follow the bearing 097° until the head of the quay is abeam, then proceed towards the anchoring area and the visitors' moorings.

Yachtsmen should note that a new light on St Mary's Pool pier head with three colour sectors has recently been installed with the object of improving night-time arrival on this approach. The characteristics are as follows: Fl.WRG.2s5m4M 070°-R-100°-W-130°-G-070° Building white roof 3m 49°55'·1N 6°19'·0W.

Approach 2

From northwest between Bacon Ledge (to the SW) and The Cow (to the NE). This is a good entrance with leading marks in line on 151°. The front leading mark is a small cream shelter with a wide vertical white stripe on a black roof. Look for a building about the size of a bus shelter. It is situated on the edge of the harbour and is not always easy to see. The rear mark is a conspicuous squat tower (37m) on the skyline on Buzza Hill. There is a stern transit for this entrance with the E edge of Hangman Island on SW edge of Carn Near (Crow Point), Tresco, on 331°. Approach on these lines until the head of the quay is abeam.

Crow Sound

Little Ganinick

Great Ganinick

Cadedna

Hats

Boiler (0₆)

Hats

Line F 284°

Line H 289°

Line BB 047°

Crow Bar

Bar Pt

Bn

Innisidgen

Trenear's Rk

Toll's I

Pelistry Bay

Vinegar Ledge

Dry Ledge

Little Britain Rk (3₂)

Great Britain Rk (8)

Gap Pt

Deep Pt

Jacky's Pt

Port Hellick Pt

Porth Hellick

Carn Friars

Normandy

Lunnon

Tremelethen

Salakee

Aero RC

Pelistry

Holy Vale

Maypole

ST MARY'S

Helvear Down

Block House Pt

Watermill Cove

Higher Trenoweth

Newford

Content

Trewince

Parting Carn

Porthloo

Control Tr

HIGH

Bant's Carn

TV TR (99)(R Lts) (119)

TELEGRAPH TR (63)

46

Toll's Porth

Carn Morval Pt

Line I 250°

Crow Rk (4₆)

BnB

Line J 207°

Line 207°

Creeb (3.7)

Approach 3 186°

Taylor's I

The Calf (1₈)

Newford I

Saint

Porth Thomas

Mary's Pool

F.R.,F.R
W,W Bn

Rat I

F.I.R.G.2s

Star Castle Hotel

Newman(2)

056°

Bacon Ledge

Approach 2 151°

The Cow (1₂)

Approach 1 097°

St Mary's Road

Woodcock Ledge (2₇)

49° 55' N

56'

TRESCO

Abbey Pool

Quay Crow Pt

Bounty Ledge

Crab's Ledge

Figtree Ledge

Yellow Ledge

Conger Ledge

Mare Ledges

(2)The Mare

Skirt I (10)

Green I (4)

Cones

Tobaccoman's Ledge

Diamond Ledge

Line S 160°

Round Rk

The Pots

Bn

Depths in Metres

HUGH TOWN

N

Quay Slip

Newford I

Customs

St Mary's Pool

Private moorings

Ferry Turning Area

Fl.RG.4M

Old Quay

Rat I

49° 55' N

6°19'W

Slip

Slip

Slip

Buzza Hill

WC

WC

F.R

x F.R

W

W

F.R

186°

151°

097°

66

0₃

6₄

3₇

3₄

0₉

0₉

3

3

20

6

1₅

1₅

0₉

2₁

18·5

Newfoundland Pt

(2₁) (1₅)

Porth Loggos

13

Church Porth

Church Pt

Church Ledges

Church Ledges

(2₄)

17

0₉

Airport

(R Lt)

Lts F.R

Inner Tolman Ledge

(0₉)

Tolman Pt

Gull Rk (1·5)

10

1₂

Gilstone Ledges

★4

(1₈)

0₃

Gilstone

(4)

Carrickstarne

(8)

6₁

Line A 241°

Line B 267°

See inset

HUGH TOWN

(48)

(38) Buzza Hill

Old Town

2₁

Old Town Bay

Carn Lêh

Dutchman's Carn

The Chair

Peninnis Head

Lt Ho ☆ Fl.20s36m12M

(15)Inner Hd

Pollard (☀)

19

31

7

0₉

Raveen

4₉ (4·6)

Porth Cressa

1₈

0₆

3

Wras (7·4)

Biggal (2·4)

8₂

0₉

14

(0₆)

65

Line C 307°

St Mary's Sound

22

ISLES OF SCILLY
St Mary's

Not to be used for navigation

N

Depths in Metres

55

32

Spanish Ledges
Bell
BYB

Spanish Ledges

✳

0₉

Little Ledge

3₄

0₉

6₄

(1₂) Round Rk

Bow Ledges

2₄

0₉

The Bow (10)

7₃ 5

Dropnose Pt

0₆

30

Line O 344°

(1₄) Cuckolds Ledge

10

4

The Hoe

GUGH

21

The Cove

16

54'

Garrison

Woolpack Pt

(0₆)

YB

3₄

(0₆)

3₁

14

Bartholomew Ledges

0₆

Fl.R.5s
R

Historic Wreck 8₅

Serica Rk

6₁

Wk (2₁)

(0₉)

Conger Ledge

(3)Steval

5₈

6°18'W

6°19'W

16'

17'

19'

Truncated   White patch on quay
roof

The line of approach from the N into St Mary's Pool on
186° (approach 3); the lower photo shows that *Scillonian*
obscures the white patch when on her berth

Guther's I.   Bab's Carn (St Martin's)   Pednbean   TV tower (St Mary's)   Pednbrose   Tean

Tean Sound, looking roughly S towards St Mary's TV
tower on 180° (line K1); Black Rock is just out of the picture
(bottom right)

Bab's Carn (St Martin's)

Pednbean

Tean Sound, looking SSE on the approach transit of 154°,
Bab's Carn (St Martin's) in line with Pednbean (line K2)

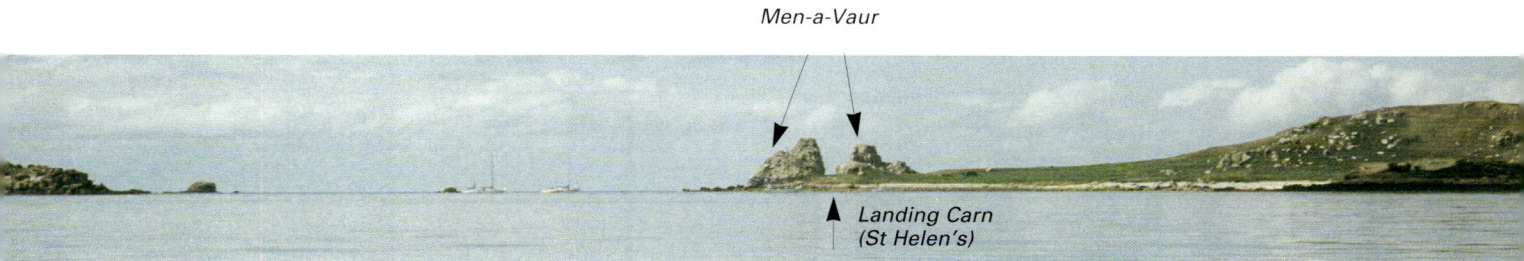

Men-a-Vaur

Landing Carn
(St Helen's)

Men-a-Vaur

Landing Carn
(St Helen's)

St Helen's Pool, looking NW; centre of Men-a-Vaur in line with St Helen's Landing Carn on 322° (line G)

Approach 3

From the north, approach on 186°, with the white patch at the head of Old Quay in line with the grey truncated roof. Note that the ferry obscures the front mark when secured alongside the New Quay. (See photos page 24.)

New navigation marks in the approaches to St Mary's

See page 14.

Approach from the north

Leading marks

Leads into Tean Sound

Line K1   TV Tower just open Goat's Point on 180°20' leads E of Black Rock

Line K2   Bab's Carn on Pednbean on 154° leads W of Black Rock

Leads S out of Tean Sound

Line L   Guther's Island on 158° with Toll's Island open to E and Innisidgen open W

Crosses the shallow flats

Line M   Green Island (Tresco) on 216°.

Leads to Hats buoy

Line G   Centre of Men-a-Vaur in line with St Helen's Landing Carn on 322° leads NW/SE to and from St Helen's Pool

Leads to Crow Rock beacon

Line S   Crow Rock beacon on TV Tower (160°31') towards St Mary's Road (see photos page 5)

Warning

As will be seen from the table on page 28, tidal streams can be strong in the approach and must be allowed for when entering, when they will be abeam.

Directions

When arriving from the N, yachtsmen should find it easy to distinguish Round Island – a noticeably hump-backed island with a conspicuous white lighthouse (55m) in the middle. This is also a very good daymark. Half a mile to starboard lies the

Guther's I.
Hedge Rock

Great Cheese Rk
Innisidgen   Foreman's I.   St Mary's   Peashopper I.

Toll's I.

St Helen's
Pool

Landing Carn
(St Helens)

Men-a-Vaur

Looking SE over Men-a-Vaur and St Helen's Landing Carn (line G), with yachts at anchor in St Helen's Pool

25

ISLES OF SCILLY
Tresco - Bryher - Samson

Not to used
for navigation

Eastward Ledge

Westward Ledge

LIGHTHOUSE
Fl.10s55m24M

24

Round I

Camber Rks

(3.6)

9₁   7₃   3₄

Didley Pt's GAP   Pollard   (1.7)

St Helen's   E Gap   Old   Man₂₈

9₁   (2.3)   4₆

TEAN

0₂

Little
Cheese   2₆
Rk

(0.7)

Pentle   1₂
Bay

2

Great
Pentle

292°

Gt Cheese Rk   (3.1)   3₇   0₆

Tea   Ledge

ST HELEN'S   42

W Gap Rk   2₉

(0.9)

Landing
Carn

6₁

6₇

Helen's
Pool

1₅   1₆

2₅

Foreman's I   Long   Ledge

Lump of
Clay Ledge   0₈   1₄

Rushy Pt   Bn⊙

Bn⊙   Lizard Pt

Bn⊙

Abbey
Hill

Tresco
Abbey

Abbey
FS

Men-a-vaur   4₆   12₈

16

*   4₃

3   3   3₅

(3.8)

Tide Rk   1₁   (1.4)

Long Pt   (0.3)

Line R   2₃   Old Grimsby
Harbour

Block House Pt

Mon   (38)

Northwethel   6₁

22

1₆

Little
Kittern   5₉

5₅   37

Old Grimsby

Bn⊙

Bn

Dolphin Town   ✠

TRESCO

(8)Golden Ball   13

Old Grimsby Sound   7₃

Line Q 124°

Merchant's Pt

Hotel   ■

Gimble
Porth   2₉

Beacon
Hill (42)

Towns
Hill

New
Grimsby

Plumb I

Abbey Hill

42

Kettle (3)   6₁

Kettle   1₈

Gimble Pt   41

Kettle Pt   31

Castle
(ruins)   ■

Cromwell's
Castle

3₆

Dunstan   0₅   🚢
Rk

Queen's Ledge   0₉

Bns   ⊙⊙   Quay

Church Quay

Plump
(2₂) Rks

Line T 157°

Kettle
Bottom   (3₂)   24

14

New Grimsby Sound   9₁

14

11

Hangman
(16)

Anneke
Quay   Bn⊙

Merrick I   1₂   *
★★★ Three
Brothers   (4₆)

Gt Crabs   (5₃)
Ledge   (2₄)

Green
Bay

68

Shipman Head   9₁

25

35   14

7₉

Shipman
Head 39
Down

Watch Hill   (43)Daymark⊙

BRYHER

The Town   Bn⊙   ✠

The Brow

Pool

27

10   1₅

14

14   1₅

Great High Rk (18)   7₈

Gweal   Porth

Merrick

Great
Porth   2₈

Gweal
Neck

Gweal
Hill   31

Stinking
Porth

Northern
(Norrard)
Rks

12₈

Gweal   29

Crow
Porth (7)

Moon Rk

• Round Rk   5₅

Eastward Ledge   11

Murr Rk(2)

Scilly
Rock   19

12   Bann Ledge 2₁

Westward Ledge   27

N Cuckoo
S Cuckoo   (17)

80

Experimental   Area

77

Black   13
Rks

31

25

Maiden
Bower

Westward
Ledge (3)

Stippit(2)

Little Maiden
Bower (13)

41°
57'
N

59'

58'

26

Skirt I
Green I
Bounty Ledge
Bn
Figtree Ledge
Broad Ledge
Yellow Ledge
Crow Pt
Conger Ledge
Paper Ledge
The Mare
Little Vincent's Ledge
Vincent's Ledge
Mare Ledges
The Pots
Abbey Pool
Appletree Pt
Carn Near
Long Crow
Chinks
Nut Rk (1.5)
Line U 340°
St Mary's Road
The Calf
The Cow
Bacon Ledge
Newman
Woodcock Ledge
Steval
Conger Ledge
Wk
Hugh Town
Porth Cressa
Star Castle Hotel
Garrison
Woolpack Pt

Lubber's Rk
Tresco Flats
Lit Rag Ledge
Gt Rag Ledge
Channel
Ledge Hulman
Bn
Stony I
Green I
Southard Well Pt
Southward Well
Great Minalto Ledges
Samson Hill
Works Pt
Yellow Rk
Puffin I
Black Ledge
Samson Flats
East Porth
North Hill
Samson
South Hill
Shag Pt
Bollard Pt
Stony Porth
Outer Colvel Rk
Long Ledge
West Porth
White I
Flea Rk
Tar Barrel Rk
Roaring Ledge
Great Minalto
Little Minalto
The Tarr
Broad Sound Ledge

Gulf Rk
Buzza Rk
Gerwick
Bream Ledge
Buzza Scud
Castinicks
Peaked Rk
Baccabu
Illiswilgig
Dollar Ledge
Castle Bryher
Flat Ledge
Middle Ledge
North Carn
Mincarlo
Biggal Ledge
Biggal
Steeple Rk

White Ground Ledge
Jacky's Rk
Picket Rk
Seal Rk
Murr Rk

North Channel

N

Depths in Metres

Tidal streams

Close N of Round Island streams begin:

Local HW	Devonport HW	Dover HW	Direction	Max rate (knots) Springs	Neaps
+0605	+0510	−0015	E	2½	−
−0020	−0115	+0545	W	2½	−

group of three tall and peculiarly symmetrical rocks called Men-a-Vaur, 19m, 31m and 35m high respectively. Just over two miles to port the St Martin's daymark can be seen in reasonable visibility. The northern landfall leads to four anchorages where a yacht may lie always afloat, namely New Grimsby Sound, Old Grimsby Sound, St Helen's Pool and Tean Sound, although St Helen's Pool is not accessible for a period either side of LWS.

The only light in this area is the powerful light on Round Island, which at night is useful for establishing that one is somewhere in the northern approaches to Scilly. However, as there are no other navigation lights or leading lights in the area, visual fixing is impossible, and night-time entry is not recommended.

The following directions are therefore for daytime approach.

New Grimsby

New Grimsby Sound leads into the gap between Tresco to port and Bryher to starboard, and is arguably the easiest entry of the four anchorages.

Buoys and beacons

Little Rag Ledge Pole beacon with red radar reflector topmark, on a small rock which dries.

Hulman Pole beacon with a green radar reflector topmark, lies on a small rock which dries.

The radar reflectors serve as topmarks. Little Rag Ledge is a cube and Hulman a triangle pointing upwards.

Leading marks

Line T W side Hangman Island on Star Castle Hotel on St Mary's on 157° leads into New Grimsby Sound

Line U Merrick Island on Hangman Island on 340° (stern transit) leads over Tresco Flats

Warning

Strong cross-tidal streams exist in the approach and must be allowed for. (See table above). Overfalls exist over Kettle Bottom which lies off N Tresco between Old and New Grimsby Sounds.

New Grimsby Harbour (Tresco)　Hangman I.　Star Castle Hotel (St Mary's)　Bryher

Entrance from N into New Grimsby Sound, with visitors' moorings (left), looking SSE; W edge of Hangman I. on Star Castle Hotel (St Mary's) on 157° (line T)

Bryher　Merrick I. Hangman I.　Carn Near (Tresco)　Tresco Abbey

Looking NW from Star Castle Hotel (St Mary's) at LW; Hangman I. with Merrick I. on 340° is the stern transit (line U) leading over Tresco Flats

Tidal streams

At the north end of New Grimsby Sound:

Stream begins:

Local HW	Devonport HW	Dover HW	Direction	Max rate (knots) Springs	Neaps	Remarks
+0440	+0345	−0140	SE	1	–	Stream changes
+0605	+0510	−0015	NW	1	–	direction four
−0320	−0415	+0245	SE	1	–	times in
+0110	+0015	−0510	NW	1	–	12 hours
Over Tresco Flats the stream begins:						
−0450	−0545	+0115	S	–	–	–
+0110	+0015	−0510	N	–	–	–

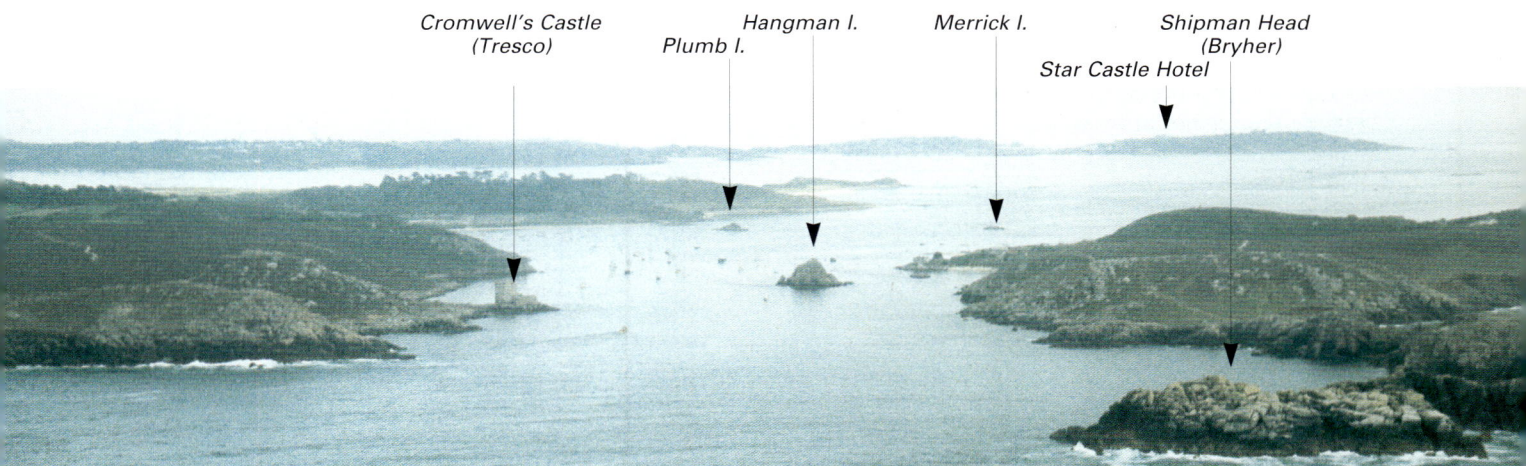

Cromwell's Castle (Tresco)   Plumb I.   Hangman I.   Merrick I.   Star Castle Hotel   Shipman Head (Bryher)

New Grimsby Sound at HW, aerial view looking SSE

Little Rag Ledge beacon   St Mary's Pool   Hulman beacon   Nut Rock

Looking SSE from Timmy's Hill (Bryher) towards St Mary's; the beacons and isolated Nut Rock can be clearly seen at LW

Directions

On the approach to New Grimsby Sound there is a transit (line T), which can be seen from well to seaward in clear visibility, formed by the right hand side of Hangman Island with the prominent building called Star Castle Hotel on Garrison Hill – the westernmost part of St Mary's – on a bearing of 157°. This transit leads clear of all the dangerous rocks on the port hand side of the sound and, once a yacht is abeam of Cromwell's Castle, the anchorage, which is nowadays full of visitors' moorings, will be clearly visible and accessible. If the above transit is not easily seen, but an approaching vessel is nonetheless sure of her position outside the entrance to the sound, then Shipman Head to starboard is quite steep-to and there are no off-lying rocks or obstructions on this side of the channel. By approaching to within 50m of the shore, close under the lee of Shipman Head, yachtsmen can quickly avoid the worst of the Atlantic swell and move out of the path of any wind from W or SW. At the same time they will be able to steer well clear of the rocks called Kettle and Kettle Bottom which extend north-westwards from the main island of Tresco. As one enters the sound, the most obvious feature is undoubtedly the pyramid-shaped 16m high Hangman Island, which stands almost in the middle of the sound and is joined to Bryher at low water. From under Shipman Head a yacht should steer toward Cromwell's Castle – the only building to be seen at that point on the Tresco shoreline. From a mid-point in the sound the visitors' moorings will open up and a course should be shaped slightly to starboard to lay the anchorage, passing equidistant from Hangman to starboard and Tresco to port.

When there is enough water, leave the anchorage at New Grimsby on a S course, passing Plumb Island 100m to port and then Merrick Island 100m to starboard. When Merrick is 300m astern steer 160° with stern transit of Merrick on Hangman (line U). Leave Little Rag Ledge beacon 50m to starboard and Hulman beacon 50m to port. Then leave Nut Rock 50m to starboard and pass into St Mary's Road.

Old Grimsby

Leading marks

Line Q   Rock 3·8m high between Merchant's Point and SW side Northwethel leads through the entrance to Old Grimsby Sound on 124° (see photos page 42)

Line R   Island Hotel on Long Point slip leads away SE from Old Grimsby Harbour clear of Blockhouse Point on 292° (stern transit)

Line S   Crow Rock beacon on TV Tower (160°31') leads towards St Mary's Road (see photos page 5)

Warning

Strong cross-tidal streams exist off the N entrance to this sound (see table page 28), and must be allowed for. Overfalls exist over Kettle Bottom off the point between Old and New Grimsby Sounds.

Directions

Although the entrance to Old Grimsby Sound shows depths between 11m at the entrance and 3·3m off Old Grimsby Harbour, there is a drying rock called Little Kittern (dries 1·9m) close abeam

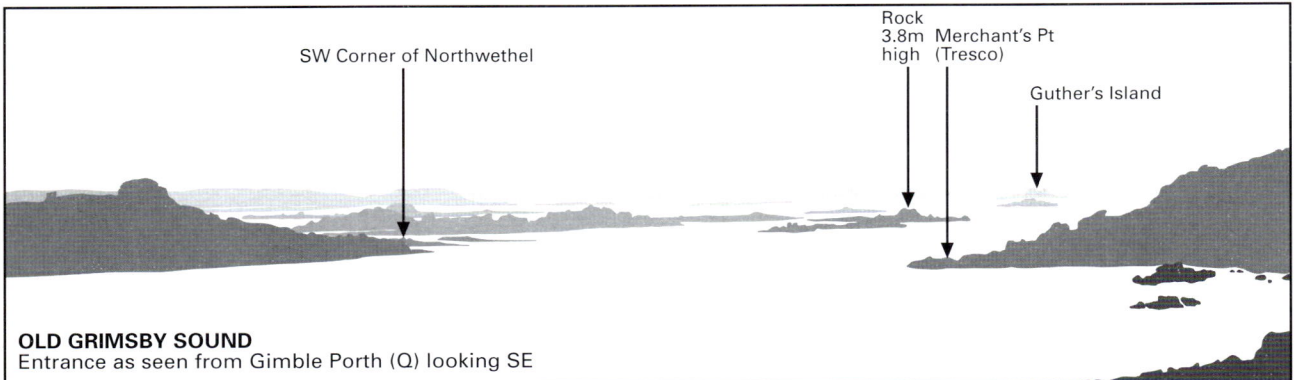

OLD GRIMSBY SOUND
Entrance as seen from Gimble Porth (Q) looking SE

Old Grimsby Sound, visitors' moorings, looking NWxN from Blockhouse Point (Tresco)

Tidal streams

Stream begins in Old Grimsby Sound:

Local HW	Devonport HW	Dover HW	Direction	Max rate (knots)		Remarks
				Springs	Neaps	
+0410	+0315	−0210	SE	–	–	Runs 8 hours
−0020	−0115	+0555	NW	–	–	Runs 4½ hours

West Gap Rock   St Helen's Gap   East Gap Rock

St Helen's Gap, looking NE from St Helen's Pool

East Gap Rock   Tean   St Mary's   West Gap Rock   Tresco

St Helen's Gap, looking S from Didley's Point (E St Helen's)

to port of the fairway in the approach. Some publications have referred to a rock called Trafford Rock at the rear of Old Grimsby Harbour which, if closed on a line of 122°, will achieve a safe arrival. No rock of this name is shown on current Admiralty charts and it is not apparently known to local boatmen. However, after an on-the-spot inspection by land and sea, it appears that the rock charted on Admiralty Chart No. *883* as 3·8m high – situated about 300m NNE of Blockhouse Point on Tresco – is the rock on which this line of bearing is based (line Q). If in doubt and time is available, it's a good idea to stand at Blockhouse Point at low water when both the 3.8m charted rock and the particularly dangerous charted Tide Rock (dries 1·4m) will be apparent – Tide Rock lying about 100m in front of the 3·8m rock. On approaching Old Grimsby from the N, navigators should visually ascertain the position of Norwethel island (22m) on the port side of Old Grimsby Sound as they enter the sound and then hold about 100m off the Tresco shore under Tregarthen Hill to starboard. As Gimble Porth opens up to starboard, they should head for the middle of the gap between Norwethel to port and Merchant's Point to starboard. At this point the features of the line of bearing (if recognised) may be followed. If not, then the line of permanent red visitors' moorings ahead can be approached directly from the middle of the gap mentioned above. Despite these mooring buoysj35, there is room to anchor both NW and SE of them. Beware of Tide Rock!

St Helen's Pool

Access to St Helen's Pool from the N is via St Helen's Gap with a minimum depth of 0.5m and a minimum width of 100m.

Tidal streams

No information is available about the streams running through this channel but they should be the same as those shown on page 28.

Directions

Leaving the E coast of Round Island about 250m to port, steer due S to hold Didley's Point – the easternmost point of St Helen's – about 100m to starboard (line N). St Helen's Gap should then bear approximately SSW between East Gap Rock (2·3m) to port and West Gap Rock (0·9m) to starboard. Approach with care to make good a course of 200° and give nothing to port until East Gap Rock is abeam. If necessary head up to West Gap Rock, as shallows and rock extend from East Gap to the NW for 50m or so. Then bear away to the S and take soundings over the shallowest part of the bar between Old Man and St Helen's (charted depth 0·5m). The rock formations constituting the East Gap and the West Gap dry to between 4·6m and 5·5m at low water springs but there is still about 3m depth between them. The sand bar begins about 200m beyond an imaginary line joining the two gap rocks, and beyond the bar there is enough water to anchor, always afloat, in almost all parts of the Pool. Although the sand bar cannot be crossed at LWS, the chart shows there is 2m of water available at St Mary's Pool at Low Water Neaps so it is likely that

71

Deep Ledges 0·6

Lion Rk (2·9)
Lion(8)
W Withan (12)
Brewer(2·9)

Eastward Ledge
Westward Ledge
Round I (41)
Fl.10s55m24M Siren (4)60s RC

Black Rk(6)
Black Rk Ledges

White I
Baker(3·8)
E Withan (14)

Men-a-vaur (35) 4·6
Camber Rks
27
South Ledge
Pernagie I
Porth Morran (1·4) 0·3

Anthony(3·7) 2·4

Golden Ball (8) (1·4)
3
4·3
6·7
Didley's Pt (1·4)
St Helen's Gap
Pollard (1·7)
Pednbrose
Plumb I 4
-3·2
41
Great Merric Ledge (5) (3·6)

Golden Ball Brow (3·6)
1·6
ST HELEN'S
W Gap Rk 5·4 (0·9)
E Gap Rk (2·3)
4·6
18
Black Porth (1·8)
Pednbean 9
Pernagie Pt 2·7
Porth Seal
4·3
St Martin's Bay

Old Grimsby Sound
49° 58' N
Little Kittern (1·9) 5·5
3·7
Northwethel 22
0·1
Crow's(17)
Foreman's (8)
3·4
30
4·2
TEAN
Old Man
5·5
Tinkler's Pt

Line Q 124°
Gimble Porth 2·9
+ 0·9
Peashopper (0·3)
0·6
Crump
1
Southward Carn
John Martin's Ledge (3·9)
Goat's Pt
Hotel Lower Town
Bab's Carn Bn
Yellow Rock
ST MARTIN'S
40

Merchant's Pt Hotel
Long Pt
Old Grimsby 2·3
Quay Bn
Tide Rk (1·4)
(3·8) 0·6
(0·9)
Line P 074°
Hedge Rk (14)
Hedge Rk Ledge
0·9
0·6
Jack's Ledge
Round Rk Ledge 1·5
Lawrence Bay
Cruther's Hill 31

Dolphin Town
Block House Pt (4·3)
Lit. Cheese Rk
(1·4) (1·4)
Lump of Clay Ledge (0·7)
1·5
Rascals Ledge (0·9)
2·5
West Broad Ledge
Stephens Ledge
Pig's Ledge
Old Quay

New Grimsby 0·8
Ember
Rushy Pt Bn
0·7
0·3
Tea Ledge 3·1
(2)
Gt Cheese Rk (3·1)
0·6
Scattering Rocks 0·1
Moth's Ledge 4·3
Parks Ledge 3·9
Wra Ledge 1·8

TRESCO
Lizard Pt
1·4
0·8
0·7
Guther's Bar 1·4
Seal Rk (1) (1·6)
(2·3) (2·4)

57'
Pentle Bay 0·7
0·8
0·4
4·1
Guther's(12) (1·6)
(1·6)
(1·5)

2·2 3·2
Abbey Hill Mon (38)
Tresco Abbey
Abbey Pool
Bn
Great Pentle Rock (1.7)
W Craggyellis (2)
E Graggyellis
0·8
0·4
Lower Ledge
1·8
2
Peaked Ledge (0·4)
Manuel Scu (1

2·8
Appletree Pt
14
Bn
Skirt I
2·3
Diamond Ledge
(0·8)
Crow Bar Sand waves
0·5
2·4
3·7
Caps
4·6

Tresco Flats
0·1
0·8 0·5
2·3
Bounty Ledge (4·4)
Crab's Ledge 0·7
Green I
3·5
Cones
Tobaccoman's Ledge
1·6
0·3
4·8
Boiler (0·6) Hats
0·4

Figtree Ledge
Broad Ledge
0·2
(0·1)
1·8
0·7
Bar Pt
3·1
8 (1·6)
1·5

Long Crow
Yellow Ledge
Crow Pt
Mare Ledges
2
1·9
2·8 Crow Rk BRB (4·6)
Bn
Innisidgen(8)
7·9

Hulman 0·3
Paper Ledge (0·3)
Conger Ledge (1·5) (1·5)
0·6
(2)The Mare
(1·5)
1·5
(1·9)
ST MARY'S
17'

2·9
56'
20'
Little Vincent's Ledge
19'
Bn
18'

Line K2 154°
Line N 182°
Line K1 180°
Line M 216°
Line G 322°
Line L 158°

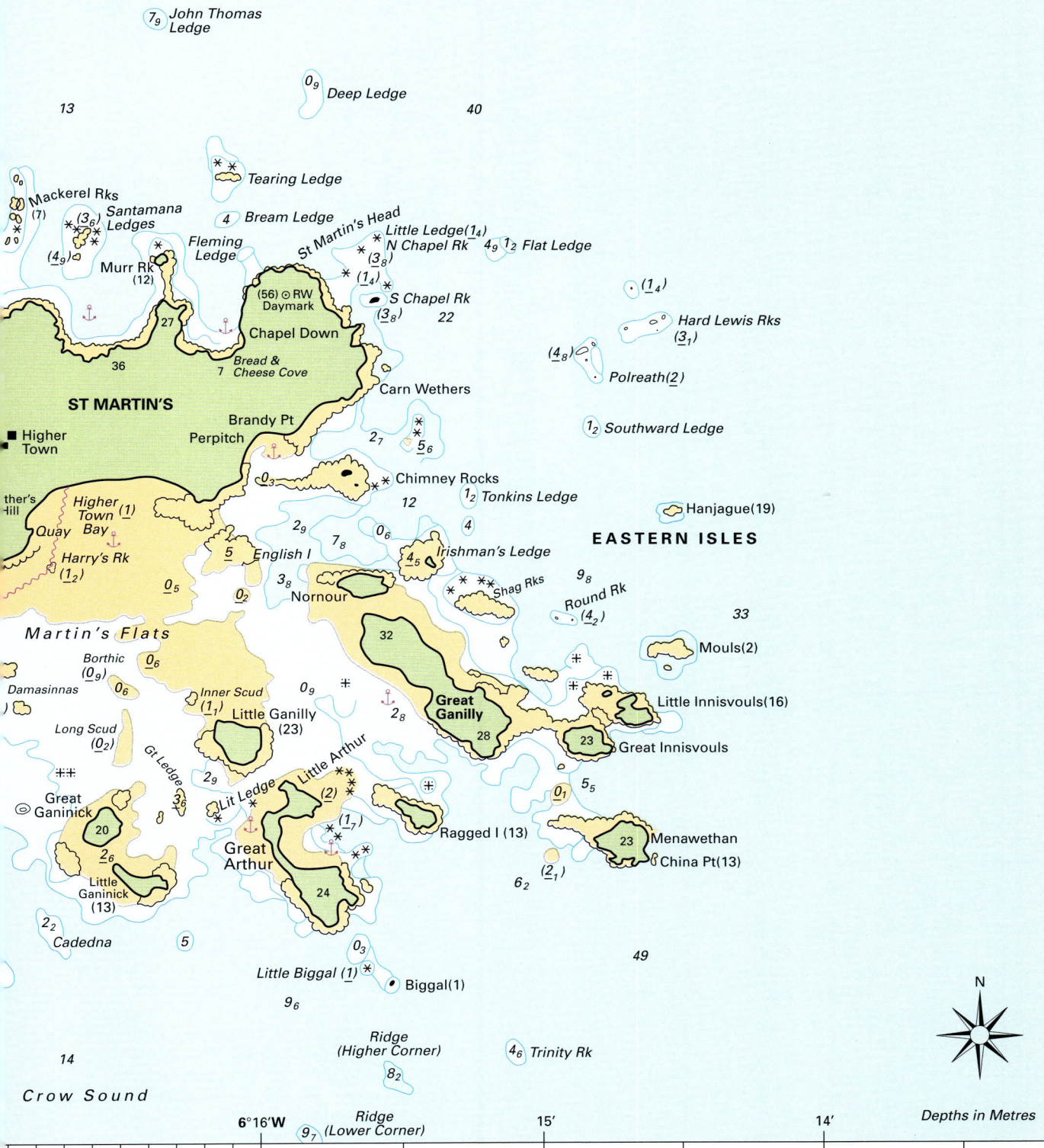

66

7_9 John Thomas Ledge

0_9 Deep Ledge

13   40

0_0 ✱✱ Tearing Ledge

0_0 Mackerel Rks
(7)
(3_6) Santamana Ledges
(4_9)
Murr Rk
(12)

4 Bream Ledge

Fleming Ledge

St Martin's Head

(3_8)
(1_4)

Little Ledge(1_4)
N Chapel Rk 4_9 1_2 Flat Ledge

(1_4)

(56) ⊙ RW Daymark

S Chapel Rk
(3_8)

22

Chapel Down

Hard Lewis Rks
(3_1)

(4_8)

Polreath(2)

27

36

Bread & Cheese Cove
7

Carn Wethers

ST MARTIN'S

1_2 Southward Ledge

■ Higher Town

Brandy Pt
Perpitch

2_7

✱
5_6

Chimney Rocks

1_2 Tonkins Ledge

Hanjague(19)

12

EASTERN ISLES

ther's Hill

Higher Town Bay
(1)

0_3

2_9 7_8 0_6 4

Quay

Harry's Rk
(1_2)

English I

4_5

Irishman's Ledge

9_8

Round Rk
(4_2)

33

0_5 0_2 3_8
Nornour

Shag Rks

Martin's Flats

32

Mouls(2)

Borthic
(0_9)

0_6

Damasinnas
0_6

Inner Scud
(1_1)

0_9

Great Ganilly

28

23 Great Innisvouls

Little Innisvouls(16)

Long Scud
(0_2)

Little Ganilly
(23)

2_8

23

Gt Ledge

✱✱

Great Ganinick

2_9

Lit Ledge

Little Arthur

(2)

✱

5_5

0_1

20

3_6

(1_7)

Ragged I (13)

23 Menawethan

China Pt(13)

2_6

Great Arthur

(2_1)

Little Ganinick
(13)

24

6_2

49

2_2

Cadedna

5

0_3

Little Biggal (1) ✱ ● Biggal(1)

9_6

14

Ridge (Higher Corner)

8_2

4_6 Trinity Rk

N

Crow Sound

6°16'W

Ridge (Lower Corner)
9_7

15'

14'

Depths in Metres

the St Helen's Gap entrance will more often than not be available – with care – to vessels drawing 1.8m. It would probably not inconvenience anyone if a yacht anchored in calm conditions in St Helen's Gap before entering St Helen's Pool after LWS when entry from the N must await sufficient water.

Tean Sound (pronounced Tee-Ann)

Tidal Streams
There is no information about the streams through Tean Sound but they should be the same as those for Old Grimsby Sound given on page 30.

Directions
The approach from seaward is strewn with rocky islets, rocks and submerged ledges. Eyeball navigation is essential, and frankly, given a choice of the other northern Scilly anchorages, one might prefer any of them even in calm conditions and good visibility. It's also best to approach Tean Sound just after low water when the hazards are most visible. There are two lines of transit (see photos page 24) of which the northwestern transit (K2), which will be described first, is the preferred route. Make for a point on a line about 500m from the E coast of Round Island and 300m from Black Rock – E x N of Round Island. Steer 154° for Pednbean rock (1·8m) in line with Bab's Carn (20m) on the W end of St Martin's until abeam of Pednbrose (12m) to starboard, at which point bear away to port in a southeasterly direction until the channel opens to the S, and then steer S on the western tip of visible land of St Martin's. Give nothing to starboard to avoid Thongyore Ledge which lies about 200m NW of Goat's Point. You may however need to borrow to starboard 100m NW of Goat's Point in order to keep the deeper water of the main channel. This course should bring a yacht into the narrow strait between Tean and St Martin's.

The northern transit (K1) offers the first possible entry into a northern Scilly harbour when arriving from the E. Observation of Round Island light approximately to the SW and St Martin's daymark approximately to the SE should assist in gaining a position due N of the entrance to Tean Sound. From here, the TV tower on St Mary's just open of Goat's Point at the W tip of St Martin's bears 180°. On the approach, alter course to SW when Lion (8m) bears SE to clear off-lying rocks and alter course after 150m to SE to pick up the transit again. When Plumb Island is abeam to port, borrow 100m to the E for 100m to clear Rough Ledge. Off Tinkler's Point follow the directions in the previous transit (see above) to steer S on the westernmost point of St Martin's.

Approach from the south
The majority of yachts visiting Scilly in recent years wear the French ensign and the southerly route is therefore the most popular. The distance from Ushant (Ouessant) or Ile Vierge on the coast of Brittany to St Mary's, Scilly, is about 100 miles and only in mid-summer in ideal conditions would most cruising yachtsmen expect to make this crossing in daylight. From S or E of Ushant, the passage is, of course, longer, and at least some of it must normally be made in darkness.

Fortunately, there is much to be said for arrival at Scilly just after dawn from this direction, given reasonable conditions of sea and visibility. The Scilly Isles are so low that they can be invisible from ten miles away, but with careful timing yachtsmen can take advantage of the excellent lights available on the southern approach, before making their entry in daylight. At dawn the islands should be well illuminated by the sun and it should be easy to pick out salient features and the main daymarks. Before dawn in fair visibility the powerful light of Bishop Rock will be seen at least twenty miles away on the port bow while Wolf Rock light will appear the same distance away on the starboard bow. After further progress towards St Mary's, both Peninnis Head light and the Seven Stones light should appear – the former dead ahead and the latter about 45° on the starboard bow – by which time Wolf Rock light will be almost abeam to starboard. Having ascertained their position on arrival off the S coast of St Mary's, yachtsmen may proceed into the southern harbours as detailed above (see page 18).

Approach from the west
For yachtsmen arriving from a westerly quadrant the wisest choice is either to go to the New Grimsby Sound approach (see page 28) or to enter from the S (see above) This decision is most likely to be based on an assessment of the probable wind direction when the yacht is eventually at anchor – the northern anchorages being more comfortable in winds from W through S, and, the southern anchorages (with the important exception of St Mary's Pool) in winds from W through N. As can be seen from the wind roses on page 7 winds from an easterly quadrant are not common in the summer months. Shelter may be obtained from such winds in all the main anchorages detailed, although swell may become a problem in The Cove and Porth Cressa if strong easterlies persist, and these places should be evacuated if the wind veers to the SE.

When arriving at the southern anchorages from the W, it is important to give Bishop Rock a wide berth. For those yachtsmen arriving from this direction for the first time, it is worth remembering that there are no points of recognition on the Retarrier Ledges, the extensive Western Rocks, Gorregan, Melledgan or Annet. The best approach tactic is to keep well clear of the area. Yachtsmen should aim to leave Bishop Rock light about 3 miles

Tidal streams

In North Channel stream begins:

Local HW	Devonport HW	Dover HW	Direction	Max rate (knots) Springs	Neaps
−0505	−0600	+0100	SE	1½	−
+0025	−0030	−0555	NW	2	−

clear to the N, at which point the white daymark on St Agnes will bear NE. (This position is only a mile E of Pol Bank with a charted depth of 23m, on which seas can break in rough or very rough weather.) Alter course to steer E and approach the land when the daymark bears N. Then bear away to the NE when St Agnes island is about a mile off and proceed to one of the anchorages. For approach to the southern anchorages see page 18.

Other approaches

North Channel, Broad Sound and Smith Sound all lie in the western approaches to the Isles of Scilly. Due to unmarked dangers, distant leading marks and the difficulty of recognising suitable reference points for navigational fixes, it is recommended that first time visitors avoid these approaches. However the following details may assist those interested in these passages. Details are also provided for the anchorage in St Mary's Road (see page 47), although this is generally not recommended as it affords little shelter to yachtsmen in any strong wind and is uncomfortable in the prevailing swell.

North Channel

This unbuoyed channel is wide and deep and presents little difficulty, but requires good visibility because the leading marks and points used for navigational fixes are distant. Tidal streams are strong and run across the line of approach. There are no suitable anchorages.

Minimum depth 10·4m, minimum width 1300m.

Leading marks

Line V   St Agnes old lighthouse between the two summits of Great Smith on 130° leads through North Channel

Line W   N summit of Great Ganilly just open N of Bant's Carn on 059° leads into St Mary's Road

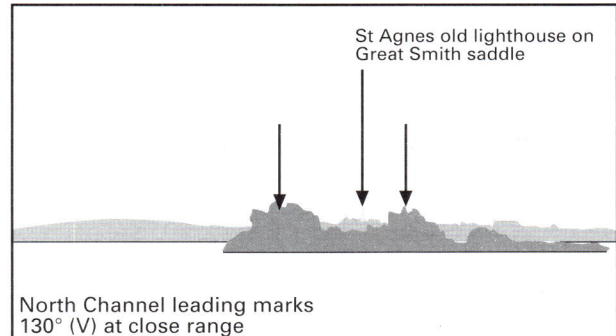

St Agnes old lighthouse on Great Smith saddle

North Channel leading marks 130° (V) at close range

Warning

Heavy breaking seas occur in gale conditions over the two 12·3m shoals located ¾M and 1M to NNW of Annet and in line with the leading marks. Overfalls occur over and near the rocky shallows to SW of this channel. There is a strong tide rip to NW of Steeple Rock during NW-going spring tides. There is a Traffic Separation Zone to NW of the approach.

Directions

Using Round Island, identified by its lighthouse, the isolated Bishop Rock lighthouse, and the old lighthouse on St Agnes, obtain a position where the latter bears 130° and Round Island is still clear N of Shipman Head, the N part of Bryher. Identify Great Smith and approach on 130° with St Agnes old lighthouse between its two summits (line V). In heavy weather borrow 500m to NE when Samson is abeam to avoid the 12·3m shoals. When ½M to N of Annet, turn onto 059° and approach St Mary's Road with the N summit of Great Ganilly just open N of Bant's Carn (line W).

Tidal streams

In Broad Sound stream begins:

Local HW	Devonport HW	Dover HW	Direction	Max rate (knots) Springs	Neaps	Remarks
−0150	−0245	+0415	ENE	½	−	The streams
+0010	−0045	−0615	SSW	1¼	−	are rotary
+0310	+0215	−0310	W	¼	−	in a clockwise
−0550	+0540	+0015	NNE	1¼	−	direction

Broad Sound

The approach from the SW is via a long straight sound which is buoyed and commences close to the easily recognised Bishop Rock lighthouse. However, the leading marks are distant and good visibility is required. There are no suitable anchorages. Tidal streams are strong in the SW part of this sound as far as Old Wreck buoy, and they sometimes set across the line of approach.

Minimum depth 13·9m, minimum width 600m.

Buoys
Round Rock N cardinal buoy, black over yellow, ✭ topmark, established about 300m to N of Round Rock (dries 2·4m).
Gunner S cardinal pillar buoy, yellow over black, ✭ topmark, marks Gunners Ledge, an awash rock 300m to N of buoy.
Old Wreck N cardinal pillar buoy, black over yellow, ✭ topmark, marks Old Wreck Rock (covers 1m) 150m to S of buoy.

Leading marks
Line W N summit of Great Ganilly just open N of Bant's Carn on 059° leads into St Mary's Road
Line X Star Castle Hotel in line with the N Haycock leads into Broad Sound entrance on 067°. Do not mistake the Ruddy (dries 4·3m, and lies 200m to WNW of the N Haycock) for the N Haycock itself

Warning
During spring tides there are heavy overfalls on either side of Broad Sound over and near the rocky shoals in the neighbourhood of Bishop Rock, Flemming's Ledge and Crim Rocks. The stream sometimes sets across the leading line until Old Wreck buoy is passed. An historic wreck is located SE of the Bishop Rock. Anchoring, fishing and diving there are prohibited (see plan pages 38-9).

Directions
Approach the Bishop Rock lighthouse on an E course, and when ¾M short of it, identify line W, or in poor visibility line X, and approach on 059° if using line W, 067° if using line X. Both of these courses leaving Flemming's Ledge to port. From here a course of 059° using line W leaves Round Rock buoy to starboard, Gunner buoy 200m to port and Old Wreck buoy close to starboard and then continues direct to St Mary's Road. When approaching Old Wreck buoy, do not stray to port: Jeffrey Rock with a charted depth of 0·9m lies about 800m approximately W of the buoy and about 400m from line W.

Smith Sound

This deep sound separates Annet from St Agnes and offers an alternative route to that of St Mary's Sound for vessels approaching from the S. The approach to the sound requires some care due to many unmarked dangers on either side of the entrance, but there are good leading marks for use in fair visibility. The sound is unbuoyed and there is a mediocre anchorage off Annet.

Minimum depth 2·5m, minimum width 200m.

Leading marks
Line Y Castle Bryher between the summits of Great Smith on 351° leads up Smith Sound
Line Z Old lighthouse on St Agnes on Penny Ledges on 091°
Line AA Carn Irish open N of Great Smith clears Halftide Ledges and Bristolman rock on 234° (stern transit)

Warning
The tidal streams from North Channel, St Mary's Sound and Smith Sound interact about 600m to N of Great Smith and should be allowed for by taking frequent navigational fixes.

Directions
Approach the old lighthouse on St Agnes on a N course, and when about 1½M from this island Great Smith will be seen through the sound. Bring this rock onto 351°, and with Castle Bryher between its summits (line Y) enter the sound. When the S point of St Agnes is abeam, borrow to E bringing Castle Bryher just E of Great Smith in order to give a good berth to Menpingrim (dries 4·8m), Buccabu (dries 1·0m) and a rock (awash) 80m to SE of Buccabu. Halfway through the sound when the old lighthouse is abeam and in line with Penny Ledges (line Z), borrow to the W of line Y and bring Castle Bryher just clear of W of Great Smith so as to avoid Pascoe Rock (covers 3m), a shoal (covers 2·5m) and the Quoins (covers 3·2m). Leave Great Smith 200m to starboard, rounding it onto a NE course towards St Mary's Road. Keep N of line AA, Carn Irish open N of Great Smith 234° (stern transit), to clear Bristolman (awash).

Tidal streams
At the N end of Smith Sound stream begins:

Local HW	Devonport HW	Dover HW	Direction	Max rate (knots) Springs	Neaps	Remarks
−0235	−0330	+0330	S	2	–	Generally in
+0225	+0130	−0355	N	2	–	direction of the sound

Tidal streams

Stream begins at entrance to Crow Sound:

Local HW	Devonport HW	Dover HW	Direction	Max rate (knots) Springs	Neaps	Remarks
−0050	−0145	+0515	W–S	1¾	¾ (SSE)	Weak, rotary anticlockwise. Max rate SSW
+0510	+0415	−0110	E–NE–N–NW	1½	½ (NE)	Max rate NE

Stream begins in Crow Sound:

Local HW	Devonport HW	Dover HW	Direction	Max rate (knots) Springs	Neaps	Remarks
−0550	+0540	+0015	N–W–SSW	½		Runs for 3 hours each way, weak and irregular at other times.
+0110	+0015	−0510	E–SSE	¾		Stream reaches 1 knot near Hats

Crow Sound

This sound is located on the NE side of St Mary's and separates it from St Martin's and the Eastern Isles. The sound has a very wide entrance and is funnel-shaped, leading to a narrow passage over Crow Bar into St Mary's Road. It is easy to locate and enter and has a good anchorage off Watermill Cove, which is untenable with winds from E–SE but sheltered from other directions, where vessels may wait for sufficient water to cross Crow Bar. The leading marks are distant and need good visibility, but the sound is buoyed and can be used with care in conditions of reduced visibility when the leading marks cannot be seen. This sound must not be used with gales from E and SE.

Minimum depth 0·8m, minimum width 150m

Buoys and beacons

Hats S cardinal yellow and black buoy with ▼ topmark, located off S edge of Hats rocky shoal (covers 0·4) plus a boiler framework (dries 0·6m).

Crow Rock Black, red, black with ⦙ topmark on an isolated rock (dries 4·6m)

Leading marks

Approach from E and ESE

Line F   Samson Hill (Bryher) on NE edge Innisidgen (N St Mary's) (284°) leads up centre of entrance

Approach from NW

Deason's Cap

Guther's I., with Deason's Cap on the W end making it a conspicuous landmark in the waters N of St Mary's

Line G   Centre of Men-a-Vaur in line with St Helen's Landing Carn 322° leads to Hats buoy (stern transit) (see photo page 25)

Crossing of Crow Bar

Line I   S end of Samson on Nut Rock and Crow Rock beacon (250°) clears Queen's Ledge

Line J   St Agnes old lighthouse on Steval (207°) leads towards St Mary's Harbour from Crow Sound

Warning

A race exists across the E entrance to Crow Sound and to the S of St Mary's, which extends up to 2M to seaward. This race occurs with the NE-going tidal stream. Local HW −0235, Devonport −0330, Dover +0330, and with strong NE wind it can be dangerous. Do not attempt, without local knowledge, to cut the corner of the entrance on the N side, especially if there is a swell which may break over shallows and shoals.

Directions

Approach Crow Sound using the leading marks (line F or line G) as required until Hats buoy is located. When it is under 1M away approach it on a WNW heading. In poor visibility, when the leading marks cannot be identified, close the NE side of St Mary's, which can always be identified by its telegraph tower, TV tower and three Decca masts, and follow the coast around to N and NW, keeping 500m from the coast and its inshore islets until Hats buoy is reached. When there is sufficient water to cross the bar, leave Hats buoy close to starboard and sail for 100m on a course of 289° towards Green Island (Tresco). This course clears the underwater rocks off Innisidgen by 100m and roughly parallels the coast. When Crow Rock beacon is seen to be on S end of Samson, turn towards it and bring the S end of Samson on to Nut Rock (line I), on course 250° crossing Crow Bar (0·8m). Crow Rock beacon can be passed on either side, but the N side is recommended. From Crow Rock beacon bring St Agnes old lighthouse on to Steval, and turn on to line J on 207°.

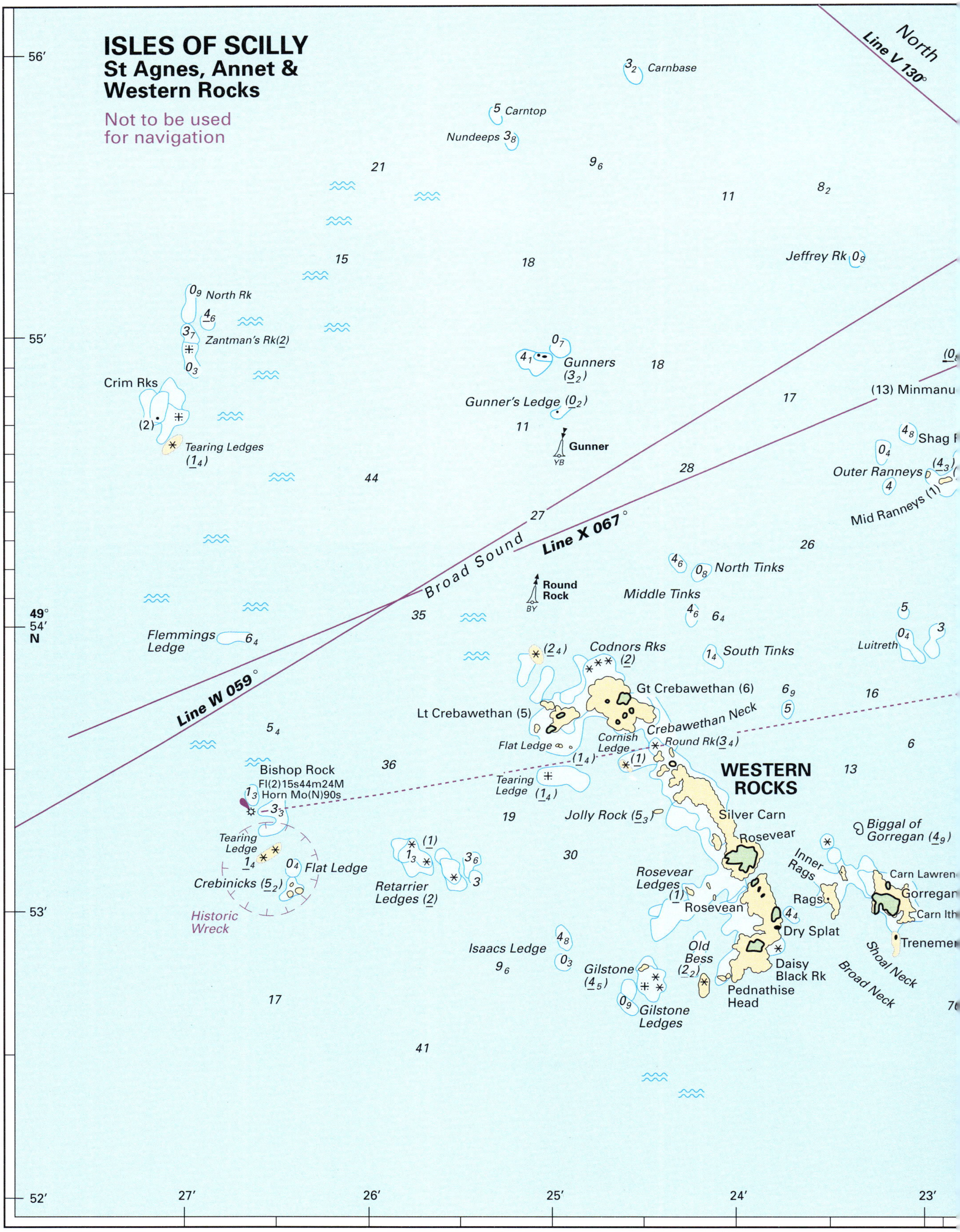

ISLES OF SCILLY
St Agnes, Annet & Western Rocks

Not to be used for navigation

North
Line V 130°

56'

3_2 Carnbase

5 Carntop

Nundeeps 3_8

21

9_6

11

8_2

15

18

Jeffrey Rk 0_9

0_9 North Rk

$\underline{4}_6$

55'

3_7 Zantman's Rk(2)

⊞

0_3

0_7

4_1 • • Gunners ($\underline{3}_2$)

18

Crim Rks

Gunner's Ledge (0_2)

17

(13) Minmanu

4_8 Shag

(2)

⊞

11

0_4

($\underline{4}_3$)

✳ Tearing Ledges ($\underline{1}_4$)

Gunner
YB

4

Outer Ranneys (1)

Mid Ranneys (1)

44

28

27

Line X 067°

26

4_6 0_8 North Tinks

Broad Sound

Round Rock
BY

Middle Tinks

4_6 6_4

5

0_4 3

35

Luitreth

49°
54'
N

Flemmings Ledge 6_4

($\underline{2}_4$) Codnors Rks
✳ ✳ (2)

1_4 South Tinks

Gt Crebawethan (6) 6_9
5

16

Lt Crebawethan (5)

Crebawethan Neck

Line W 059°

5_4

Cornish Ledge

Round Rk($\underline{3}_4$)

WESTERN ROCKS

13

Flat Ledge ∞ (1_4)

(1)

6

36

Bishop Rock
Fl(2)15s44m24M
1_3 Horn Mo(N)90s
✳ ⊹ 3_3

Tearing Ledge ($\underline{1}_4$)

⊞

19

Silver Carn

Jolly Rock ($\underline{5}_3$)

Rosevear

Biggal of Gorregan ($\underline{4}_9$)

Tearing Ledge $\underline{1}_4$

0_4 Flat Ledge

(1)
1_3

3_6

30

Inner Rags

Carn Lawren

Crebinicks ($\underline{5}_2$)

Retarrier Ledges ($\underline{2}$)

3

Rosevear Ledges

Rosevean

Rags

Gorregan

Carn Ith

53'

Historic Wreck

Isaacs Ledge

4_8

Dry Splat

4_4

Treneme

9_6

0_3

Gilstone ($\underline{4}_5$)

Old Bess (2_2)

Daisy Black Rk

Shoal Neck

Broad Neck

⊞ ✳

0_9 Gilstone Ledges

Pednathise Head

17

41

52'

27'   26'   25'   24'   23'

Channel

Broad Sound Ledge
Spencers Ledge

Line C 307°
Line BB 041°
Line AA 234°

Woodcock Ledge

Star Castle Hotel
Hugh Town
ST MARY'S

(3)Steval

Garrison Hill

Conger Ledge

Woolpack Pt
Porth Cressa
The Wras

Old Wreck Rk

N Bartholomew
Fl.R.5s
Bartholomew Ledges
Historic Wreck

YB Woolpack
Biggal(1)
(10)The Chair
(15)Inner Hd
Lt Ho Fl.20s 36m12M

Pollard
Peninnis Head

Bristolman
Little Bristolman
Halftide Ledges
Teneers Ledge
Perconger Ledge
Little Perconger

Spanish Ledges

Ruddy Sharks Fin
Haycocks(18)
Gt Smith
Round Rk
The Cow
Kittern Rk(17)
Gulf Pt
The Bow
Bow Ledges

BYB Spanish Ledge Bell

St Mary's Sound

Annet Hd
Tins Walbert
Porth Coose
Kittern Hill
GUGH

manueth
Carn Irish
ANNET
Carn Windlass
Periglis
Big Pool
Old Lt Ho
ST AGNES

Round Rk
Little Ledge

hag Rks

Inner Ranneys
Pascoe Rk
Penny Ledges
Line Z 091°
St Warna's Cove
Dropnose Pt
Cuckold's Carn
Cuckold's Ledge

Annet Ledge
Custom House Rk(3)
Annet Neck
Menglow
Menrounds
The Cove
The Hoe

Hellweathers Neck
(5)South Carn
Buccabu(1)
Western Rk
Ragged Rk
Little Hakestone
Wingletang Bay

Hale Rk (6)
Isinvrank(4)
Brothers (32)
Menpingrim
Lethegus Rks
Pidney Brow
Great Wingletang(2)
Wingletang Ledges

Muncoy Neck
Muncoy
Little Menbean
Great Menbean
Smith Sound

Seal Rk
Menfleming(2)
Flat Carn(2)
Melledgan(7)

Biggal
Little Stone
Gorregan Neck

arn Ithen

Line Y 351°

N
Depths in Metres

6°22'W
21'
20'
19'
18'

III. Anchorages

1. Main anchorages

New Grimsby Sound (Tresco)

Sheltered N–NE–E–SE–S–SW–W

At HW the anchorage can become uncomfortable with strong S–SSW winds and swell, and can become rough with strong NW winds and swell.

The anchorage lies on a NW/SE line between Hangman Island and Frenchman's Point to the NW and a line joining the yellow mark NW of New Grimsby Harbour quay and the similar yellow mark on the shore under Watch Hill, Bryher. These two yellow marks show where not to anchor owing to buried transmission lines. Depths in the anchorage vary from about 5m in the NW to about 2m in the SE. The bottom is sand and gravel. At Springs the tide runs at 2 knots or more. There are now 16 orange visitors' mooring buoys laid in the anchorage on the Tresco side of the channel, thereby somewhat restricting space available for fin-keel vessels to anchor. However, with care, space can be found in the westerly part of the anchorage; the fee for anchoring is £5. The overnight charge for a visitor's mooring is £10 per 24 hours and the fee is collected by the Tresco harbourmaster, Henry Birch – sometimes in the early evening and sometimes in the morning. The visitors' moorings are heavy-duty and, except in the direst weather conditions, offer reliable security to properly moored vessels. Visitors supply their own mooring strops for these buoys and in strong NW winds would be wise to back up rope strops with chain strops and shackles. One problem in this anchorage is the extensive Japanese seaweed which is particularly rife at low water. If using the engine to charge the batteries, weed can entirely block the outer access to the engine cooling water intake. While charging, check exhaust!

Dinghy access to Tresco can be had, with sufficient rise of tide, anywhere on the shore within New Grimsby Harbour. As in all Scilly harbours, visitors' dinghies are not allowed to be secured alongside the protective quay, which is used by ferries and commercial vessels. There is room for one medium-size yacht to dry out alongside the

New Grimsby Sound, with visitors' moorings, looking S from King Charles Castle (Tresco)

... e of submarine cables Dinghies may be left on shore   Post office   Entrance to drying harbour

New Grimsby (Tresco), looking E from visitors' moorings

Shipman Head (Bryher)
(Tresco)

Cromwell's Castle
(Tresco)

New Grimsby Sound in a blow, looking NW

inshore part of the harbour quay provided permission has been granted by the harbourmaster. In the season, the seaward end of the quay is extremely busy with tourist traffic during daylight hours. There is a tap at the rear of the post office at the root of the quay at New Grimsby Harbour, from which fresh water is available to be carried in ship's plastic containers. New Grimsby Harbour dries, is full of private moorings and is not open to visiting yachts, even if they can take the ground.

New Grimsby anchorage also gives convenient access Bryher. At high water, ferries use the stone quay close to Bryher church but at other times they use the pontoon extending from The Bar opposite New Grimsby quay. This is the most convenient dinghy landing point but dinghies should not be secured in such a way as to obstruct ferry access.

Old Grimsby Harbour (Tresco)

Sheltered E–SE–S–SW–W–NW–N–NE

The anchorage lies between an imaginary line joining the charted Island Hotel with the S end of Norwethel and a point about 150m NE of Blockhouse Point, marking the SE end of the harbour. Within this area there are six red visitors' moorings for which overnight charges are payable to the Tresco harbourmaster. There is, however, a fair amount of room for fin-keel yachts to anchor within the suggested boundaries and there is still water to about 2·5m depth SE of Tide Rock. The bottom is mainly sand and gravel. SE of Tide Rock, anchors need to be set with care. If in doubt re-anchor with sufficient scope until you are happy. At Springs the tide can run at over 2 knots.

Fees are the same as for New Grimsby. Dinghies can be landed on the beach.

St Helen's Pool (St Helen's)

Sheltered N–NE–E–SE–S–SW–W–NW

Although it's only about a half mile dinghy trip to Old Grimsby Harbour (depending on the state of the tide), this anchorage offers seclusion, fine views and good holding in 2m to 7m sand for those folk prepared to put up with a complete lack of nearby facilities. The roadstead was once used by quite large vessels and although one cannot describe the pool as landlocked, the islands, rocks and banks around it do in fact create this effect except at high water when, in the prevailing westerlies, the Atlantic breaks across the rocks of Golden Ball Brow to the NW; even then these extensive rocks afford some shelter from the outside swell and the tide flows more slowly in most parts of the pool than in other more restricted Scillonian anchorages. If, while in St Helen's Pool, the wind blows up from any direction, one can move to other more protected parts of the pool in the lee of land or rocks. The anchorage is sheltered from all directions at low water, but strong winds from the NW, NE, and SE may produce

Merchant's Point (Tresco)   Slick over Tide Rock   Norwethel

Old Grimsby Sound, with visitors' moorings, looking NW

Crow's I.   Round I. light   St Helen's   Didley's Point   West Gap Rock
                                                      (St Helen's)   Forema

Peashopper

Rock 3·8m

Looking NxE towards St Helen's from Blockhouse Point
(Tresco); rock 3·8m is the constituent of line Q for entering
Old Grimsby from the NW on 124°

uncomfortable conditions and some swell, more
especially around high water. Yachtsmen may wish
to take anchor bearings, in which case the church
tower at Dolphin Town on Tresco to the SW, the
landing carn on the W end of St Helen's, and the
conspicuous Hedge Rock to the SE are useful in
most parts of the pool. In some parts of the pool,
Round Island light can be seen to the N behind St
Helen's island.

Golden Ball   Golden Ball Brow   Men-a-Vaur   Landing Carn (St Helen's)

St Helen's Pool looking NW

Tean Sound (St Martin's)

Sheltered NE–E–SE–S–SW–W–NW
Subject to swell

This sound forms the seaway between Tean and St Martin's and, at its narrowest point, the gap between the low water rocks is only about 100m. Charted depths in the sound between Thongyore Ledge and Southward Carn (the SW point of St Martin's) are, from N to S, 5·5m, 8·2m, 8·2m and 7·3m. So it's quite deep and furthermore the bottom is mainly rock. In the deep water the St Martin's Hotel has installed seven moorings for the use of visiting yachts. Visitors who utilise the hotel's restaurant do not have to pay for an overnight mooring. Otherwise the charge is £10. Yachtsmen determined to anchor should ensure their ground tackle can cope with the rock bottom, the spring flow of 2 knots or more and the need for a lot of scope on anchor chains. Swell can also be a problem. Don't obstruct the quay or leave your dinghy on it, but use the beach.

St Mary's Pool (St Mary's)

Sheltered NE–E–SE–S–SW

On arrival in the pool you may pick up a visitor's mooring if there is a vacancy. It is courteous to report to the harbourmaster's office as soon as you can, although the staff may be fully occupied when the ferry *Scillonian* arrives from the mainland. Contact the harbourmaster on VHF Ch 16 and then go to working Ch 14.

The 38 visitors' mooring buoys now occupy much of the area formerly available for yachts to anchor. However, the holding in this area was never very good and it was well known for vessels to drag as soon as the wind veered through W to NW following the usual pattern on the passing of a deep depression. As these moorings are heavy-duty – the two seaward lines of moorings are for 60' vessels and the rest for 40' vessels – yachtsmen using them may find their vessels are safer than previously in this anchorage. Visitors may have to share one of the mooring buoys, quite possibly with commercial vessels, when there is heavy demand for shelter in bad weather. The charge for overnight use is £10 and the harbour staff visit vessels each morning to collect fees.

There is one stumbling block. In strong W to NW winds, vessels on these moorings naturally lie back and, if there is a vacancy on the mooring astern, then a yacht of 35' or more may well bump regularly into that mooring buoy. Many people think this a small price to pay for the relative safety of the anchorage and the avoidance of the inconvenience of moving elsewhere. Of course, yachts will lie more easily as the depression passes through.

There is still room to anchor to the W of the visitors' moorings near the lifeboat and the customs buoy, but be careful not to anchor NE of the quayhead in the area used by the ferry *Scillonian* as turning space. Anchoring is not encouraged and is subject to the same £10 fee.

The harbour plan (see page 23) shows the large area occupied by private moorings. Almost half of this area – on the landward side between the quay and the lifeboat slip – dries at low water neaps and the drying part extends almost to the end of the New Quay at springs. Dinghies, secured on long lines, may be left only at the corner of the New Quay and the Old Quay. If they are left elsewhere, they may be surreptitiously moved. The harbour staff are usually happy to grant permission for vessels to dry out against the quay just N of the dinghy mooring – usually for the purpose of making some repair. Occasionally, demand for this berth necessitates rafting. Long warps are required and crew need to adjust them as tidal height changes.

Diesel fuel is available from a portable pump at the N end of the main quay in the position where the *Scillonian* secures alongside, every day except Sundays. Fresh water is also available from the same spot. *Scillonian* is never alongside between 0800 and 1100 (except occasionally at weekends in August) and the harbour staff will be pleased to serve your

St Martin's Hotel (St Martin's)

Tean Sound, with visitors' moorings, looking NE

Harbourmaster's   Lifeboat   New Quay   Old Quay   Old lifeboat slip
office (Rat I.)   station

St Mary's Pool (St Mary's) at HW (top) and LW (bottom), looking NE from near Star Castle Hotel; visitors' moorings extend beyond the lifeboat and occupy most of the available deep water

requirements for fuel and water at this time. It's wise to get there early as a queue soon forms during the season. Except for a tap at New Grimsby (see page 41) there is no public availability of fresh water convenient for yachtsmen anywhere else in Scilly.

Those yachtsmen thinking of visiting other islands would do well to spend some time in St Mary's, first checking out the three transits on the approach to the harbour (as the components of each transit can all be seen with a little effort), and then walking up to the Star Castle Hotel, and checking out the lie of the land from the battlements. It is best to do this at LW and ideally at Springs when great stretches of sand appear. It is a salutary exercise to envisage how one can walk (perhaps run would be a better word!)

between the islands at LWS (except for Gugh/St Agnes which have always been separated by deep water from the rest of the inhabited islands).

A trip on one of the local boats can also be a good way to familiarise oneself with marks and channels, before exploring the other islands in one's own vessel.

Porth Cressa (St Mary's)
Sheltered W–NW–N–NE–E

This is a pleasant anchorage offering good shelter in strong NW winds and convenient access to Hugh Town, although it's a long haul by dinghy from the seaward anchor berths to the town at HW. The very

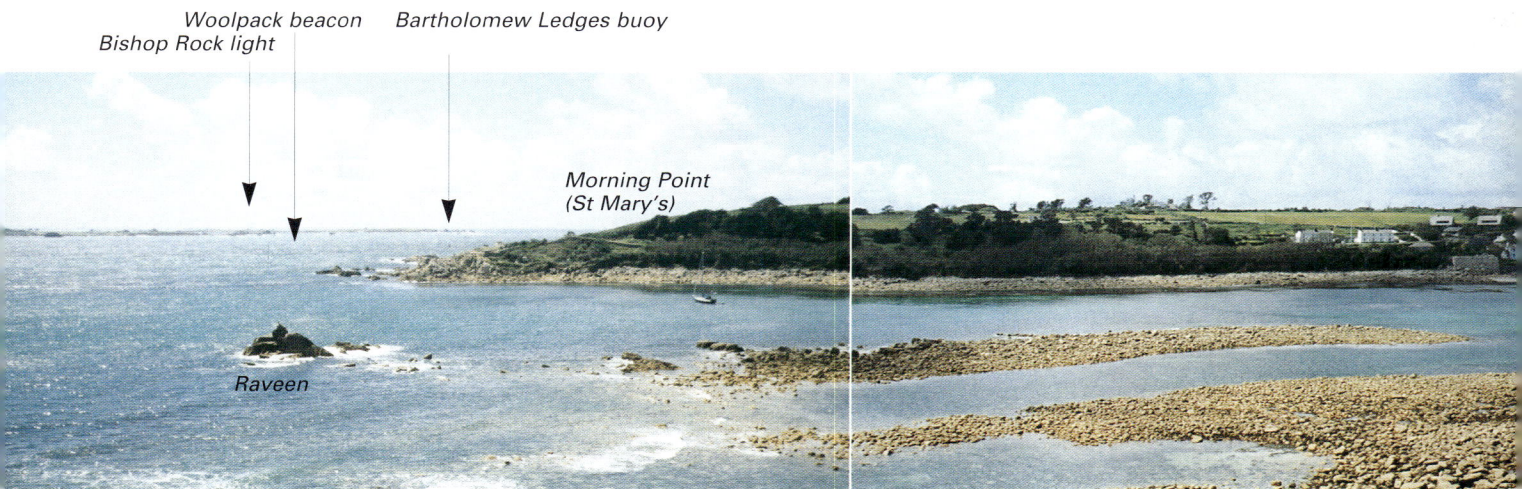

Bishop Rock light
Woolpack beacon
Bartholomew Ledges buoy
Morning Point
(St Mary's)
Raveen

Porth Cressa (St Mary's), panoramic view from above E side of the harbour

Raveen
Biggal   Wras
Morning Point (St Mary's)

Porth Cressa towards LW, looking roughly S

Hat's buoy
St Martin's
Great Ganinick
Little Ganinick

Watermill Cove (St Mary's), looking NE from the boathouse above the bay

limited area of sheltered deep water for fin-keel yachts lies between Raveen and Morning Point, and extends about 200 metres into the harbour, which is otherwise shallow or drying. Swell can be unpleasant in Porth Cressa and it is time to leave if wind arrives from a southerly quadrant. The bottom is sand with rocky patches and depths vary from about 7m W of Raveen to 2m 150m to the NW.

Watermill Cove (St Mary's)

Sheltered S–SW–W–NW

This anchorage is situated on the NE coast of St Mary's and offers fin-keel yachts particularly good shelter in SW winds. Approach on a southwesterly course and tuck in with care among some rocky patches to find anchorage in about 5m sand. There is not much room close in at Watermill Cove but, provided the wind does not shift to NW one can still find shelter in about 10-12m further offshore. It's also a good spot to wait for sufficient rise of tide over Crow Bar, if wanting to make St Mary's Pool round the N of the island.

Innisidgen

Watermill Cove, looking NW from the Boat House above the bay

The Cove (St Agnes & Gugh)

Sheltered SW–W–NW–N–NE–E

There is good anchorage in sand 2m towards the head of The Cove and good deeper water about halfway up in about 7m. There is usually plenty of room and 20 yachts should present no problem. When The Bar covers at HW, quite a strong set develops to the SE. At this time it is dangerous to bathe on the bar. Otherwise the bathing is excellent. The Cove is probably the easiest of the southern anchorages to enter when arriving at Scilly by the southern approach.

Porth Conger (St Agnes and Gugh)

Sheltered in winds from NE–E–SE–S–SW

This anchorage is situated on the other side of the bar which separates Gugh and St Agnes. This anchorage is not particularly recommended because there are permanent private moorings, there is little

St Agnes *The Bar* *The Cow* *Gugh*

The Cove, between St Agnes and Gugh, looking NW

St Agnes *The Cow* *Porth Conger* *The Bar* *Gugh*

The Cove, looking N towards Porth Conger

room for visitors, the holding is not very good and the anchorage becomes open to wind and sea as soon as a normal depression passes through. However, for a short stay the anchorage is quite pretty and there is a good beach. There is a small landing quay, many ferries in the season and a lot of visitors. Enter on a SE heading between The Cow and St Agnes and anchor when the hill called Kittern on Gugh bears E. Depth 2m or less.

2. Other anchorages

There follows a list of anchorages which, for the reasons stated on page 000, are not generally suitable as destinations for fin-keeled yachts and are only likely to be of interest to shoal-draught vessels in very settled weather. The anchorages are given island by island and are generally only to be recommended for a daytime stop. Latitude and longitude are given for these minor anchorages to help readers locate them on large-scale charts. These positions should not be used for navigation.

St Mary's

St Mary's Road

This anchorage, which lies near the centre of the group of islands, is the main anchorage for larger vessels in depths of up to 15m. It is available as an anchorage for yachts and smaller vessels in winds from NW–N–NE–E, but it becomes very uncomfortable with any swell from the SE–S–SW–W and dangerous under SW gale conditions, when even large ships may have to seek shelter in the lee of St Mary's island. Yachts can also find shelter in Porth Cressa or New Grimsby Sound.

Leading marks
BB St Martin's Daymark on summit of Creeb on 041° clears Woodcock Ledge

Warning
In the event of SW or W winds arising, yachts should leave this anchorage and proceed to New Grimsby Sound or to Crow Sound. A network of cables crosses between St Mary's and Tresco in the area of Crow Bar and between the larger islands (see plan pages, 20-21).

Old Town Bay
49°54'·6N 06°18'·00W
Sheltered SW–W–NW–N–NE
The original harbour for St Mary's, which dries.

Gull Rk   Gilstone   Carn Lêh
St Mary's)

Old Town Bay looking SE

Old Town Bay (St Mary's), looking SE

The entrance requires great care owing to dangers on either hand. Enter on a NW course 80m from Tolman Point. There is an anchorage in 3m sand and rock in the entrance which is exposed, otherwise dry out further inshore. A small village with two cafés. There is a church at the head of the bay, and the airport control tower is ¼M to E. The head of the harbour is occupied by the moorings of the Old Town Boat Club. The W side of the head of the harbour is foul and there is an old quay and slip on the E side.

Tidal streams
In St Mary's Road stream begins:

Local HW	Devonport HW	Dover HW	Direction	Max rate knots		Remarks
				Springs	Neaps	
−0550	+0540	+0015	E	1	–	Constant direction
−0050	−0145	+0515	SW–W–NW	¾	–	Direction varies

47

Hats SE and NW

Sheltered S–SW–W–NW–N

The deep-water anchorages used by large vessels when there is a SW gale. Anchor in 5 to 12m sand 400m to SE and also 1000m to NW of Hats yellow and black S cardinal buoy, ⊻ topmark.

Porth Hellick and Porth Loggos

49°54'·90N 06°17'·00W and
49°54'·75N 06°16'·88W
Sheltered SW–W–NW–N–NE

Porth Hellick is a drying anchorage, difficult to enter and only suitable for small craft. It is relatively deserted. Only enter in good conditions, on a NW heading from Porth Hellick Point. Sir Cloudesley Shovell's grave and a Bronze Age burial chamber are nearby (Sir Cloudesley Shovell was later reburied in Westminster Abbey). The beach is famous for its shells. Heavy dangerous swell with onshore winds. An alternative but exposed anchorage is in Porth Loggos, just W of Newfoundland Point in 6m rocks and sand.

Pendrathen

49°56'·10N 06°18'·10W
Sheltered E–SE–S–SW–W

A drying anchorage, easy to enter on a SE heading, which is used as a mooring area by small craft. Wras, a rocky patch (dries 5m), marked by a pole, lies in the centre of the area. There is a cable beacon with yellow ◆ topmark at Bar Point and a ruined jetty at the opposite end of the small bay.

Toll's Porth

49°55'·80N 06°18'·50W
Sheltered NE–E–SE

Small drying anchorage, rocky bottom. Ancient village and Bant's Carn burial chamber nearby ashore.

Porth Loo

49°55'·30N 06°18'·50W
Sheltered N–NE–E–SE–S

A large drying anchorage with sand and rock bottom, easy to enter on an E heading. A small collection of houses ashore.

Porth Thomas/Shark's Pit

Sheltered N–NE–E–SE–S

A small drying anchorage in the NE corner of St Mary's Pool with sand and rock bottom. Standing stone on top of Mount Flagon, adjacent to leading mark.

St Martin's

Higher Town Bay

49°57'·45N 06°16'·65W
Sheltered W–NW–N–NE

An open bay anchorage with a sandy bottom that dries and is easy to approach. There is a fine sandy beach. Higher Town with its shop and post office lies on the hill above the anchorage. Some isolated rocks.

Perpitch

49°57'·55N 06°16'·00W
Sheltered W–NW

A small anchorage which needs care in entering because of off-lying rocky shoals. Approach on a SW course and anchor in 1·5m sand. Small sandy beach; normally deserted.

Stony Porth/Bread and Cheese Cove

49°57'·85N 06°16'·20W
Sheltered E–SE–S–SW–W

An anchorage with rocky sides and an approach which needs care. Approach on a SW or SE course to avoid Tearing Ledge. Anchor in 5m sand and rock. Normally deserted.

Bull's Porth

49°57'·85N 06°16'·45W
Sheltered E–SE–S–SW–W

An anchorage with rocky sides which needs care on the approach. This should be on a SSW heading leaving Murr Rock 100m to port. Anchor in 5m sand. The cove is usually deserted.

St Martin's Bay

49°58'·00N 06°17'·15W
Sheltered E–SE–S–SW–W–NW

A wide bay with several anchorages which need great care in the approach between the many rocky ledges. Approach on a S course leaving Great Merrick Ledge 150m to starboard and then Mackerel Rocks 150m to port. Anchor in 3m sand. Large sandy beach which usually has some visitors.

Porth Morran

49°58'·50N 06°17'·55W
Sheltered NE–E–SE–S–SW–W

An anchorage behind islands which offers best shelter at LW. The approach requires care and should be made on a S heading leaving White Island 200m to port. Anchor in 3m sand and rock. White Island is often visited by tourists. Stony beach and shallow caves.

Lawrence's Bay

49°57'·60N 06°17'·40W
Sheltered W–NW–N–NE–E

A drying anchorage really only suitable for very shallow-draught craft, with local knowledge, owing to the large number of rocky shoals on the approach.

Tresco

Rushy Porth

49°57'·25N 06°19'·25W
Sheltered S–SW–W–NW–N–NE

A drying anchorage off the beach. Approach by Old Grimsby Sound (see page 30). Amount of shelter depends on the height of tide. Usually deserted. Cables come ashore near centre of porth and at Rushy Point where there are beacons with yellow ♦ topmarks.

Green Porth/Raven's Porth
Old Grimsby Harbour

49°57'·55N 06°19'·85W
Sheltered E–SE–S–SW–W–NW–N–NE

These two porths are separated by a projecting quay and together form Old Grimsby Harbour. Approach by Old Grimsby Sound (see page 30) and enter on a W heading. The area is shallow and dries at LWS. Alternative anchorage is in 2·5m sand, 300m to NE of the quay. The amount of shelter depends on the height of tide and actual position. There is a cable which runs across Green Porth where anchoring is prohibited. This harbour is now only used by a few fishing boats, but was very busy in the past. Landing can be made on the sandy beach. Strong tidal streams. The long narrow dinghy slip to N of Raven's Porth is the private property of the Island Hotel. There are moorings near the centre of the harbour.

Gimble Porth

49°57'·80N 06°20'·30W
Sheltered NE–E–SE–S–SW–W

A rather exposed anchorage in a wide bay approached by Old Grimsby Sound (see page 30). Enter on a S course towards the centre of the bay.

Green Porth   Raven's Porth

Old Grimsby Harbour (Tresco)

Anchorage in 2m sand just inside the line joining the two arms of the bay. A drying anchorage is available further inshore. Keep a sharp look-out for rocks and stones. Usually deserted.

Castle Porth

49°57'·65N 06°20'·90W
Sheltered N–NE–E–SE–S–SW–W

A small anchorage tucked away to the S of Cromwell's Castle, suitable for smaller vessels but subject to swell. Many visitors ashore.

Bryher

Great Popplestones

49°57'·20N 06°21'·65W
Sheltered NE–E–SE–S–SW

A dangerous but fascinating anchorage, for use only in very settled conditions by experienced yachtsmen. There is a stony bar across the entrance which is very narrow. Approach on a SE course. Enter on an ESE heading and anchor in 1·5m sand and stones. Most of the anchorage dries at LWS. Beach of sand and rock.

Stinking and Great Porths

49°56'·90N 06°21'·60W
Sheltered NE–E–SE–S–SW

Two anchorages for use in very settled weather; both coves dry at their heads, but Great Porth has 1·5m sand some 200m from the head of the cove. Approach keeping Scilly Rock on a stern bearing of 320° and enter either cove on an ENE course with great care. A wide sandy beach with rocks. Both are dangerous anchorages with onshore winds or swell.

Stony Porth and South Stony Porth

49°56'·68N 06°21'·50W

These two anchorages are not recommended to visitors. They require considerable care in the approach and entrance because of numerous rocks and, like those described above, can only be used in settled weather. Local knowledge is essential.

Rushy Bay

49°56'·55N 06°21'·10W
Sheltered W–NW–N–NE–E–SE–S

An anchorage in 2m sand, off a beautiful beach but rather exposed, for use only in settled weather. Approach with Works Point, the S end of Bryher, on 050°, with care because of isolated rocks. Anchorage 200m to S of Works Point. There are other anchorages nearby.

Green Bay (Bryher)

Green Bay

49°57'·00N 06°21'·00W

This anchorage is not suitable for fin-keel yachts unless they are equipped with legs, as the anchorage always dries. However, for vessels which can take the ground, Green Bay offers valuable shelter from all except SE winds. Green Bay may be approached with sufficient rise of tide by using Merrick Island as a stern bearing on 080°.

Samson

Bar Point

49°56'·32N 06°21'·00W
Sheltered N–NE–E–SE–S–SW

Anchor in 2m sand 200m to N of Bar Point, very exposed. Only for use in settled weather. Approach with Works Point (Bryher) on 050° with care and when Outer Colvel Rocks (Bryher) are abeam, approach on a SE heading leaving Bollard Point 200m to starboard.

West Porth

49°56'·00N 06°21'·40W
Sheltered N–NE–E–SE–S

Another anchorage for use only in very settled weather, with an approach which needs considerable care. Approach as above with Works Point 050°, and when the saddle of Samson is due E, approach leaving White Island 100m to starboard. Anchor in 1·5m sand and rock 300m offshore. Often heavy swell from W–SW.

East Porth

49°55'·95N 06°21'·00W
Sheltered S–SW–W–NW

A drying anchorage approached on a NW heading leaving Green Island off Samson 100m to starboard. Sand and rock, sandy beach. Only suitable for shallow craft in very settled weather. At HW this anchorage is exposed to swell from S. There are many rocks in the approach.

Bar Point (Samson)   New Grimsby (Tresco)   Puffin I

The anchorage off Bar Point (Samson), looking NxE from South Hill above

Looking SxW from New Grimsby Sound; a yachtsman has
misjudged the falling tide over Tresco Flats

St Agnes and Gugh

Dropnose Porth

49°53'·60N 06°19'·55W
Sheltered S–SW–W–NW

A shallow, rather open anchorage to E of Gugh with
very difficult approach and entrance. Should not be
attempted without local knowledge.

Porth Killier

49°53'·75N 06°20'·62W
Sheltered SE–S–SW–W

A drying anchorage, with a narrow entrance and two
rocks in the centre, for use in settled weather with
care. The bottom is rocky with sand patches in
places. Usually deserted.

Porth Coose

49°53'·80N 06°21'·16E
Sheltered NE–E–SE–S–SW

An anchorage in 1·5m sand and rock that requires
great care in the approach and entrance and, subject
to swell, should only be used in settled weather.
Enter on a SW heading on to Little Smith and S of
Great Smith and Halftide Ledges. When the old
lighthouse is SE turn and enter. Normally deserted.

Periglis

49°53'·60N 06°21'·00W
Sheltered N–NE–E–SE–S–SW–W

A drying anchorage for use with care. Enter on an E
heading 50m to N of Penny Ledges and anchor
near, but clear of, the permanent moorings. Two
broken slips on the shore shaped like an inverted 'Y'

The harbour at Periglis (St Agnes), looking NE

Great
Innisvouls   Menawethan   Great Ganilly   Nornour   Ragged I.   Great Arth

The Eastern Isles, looking SxE from St Martin's daymark

for use by dinghies in calm weather. An alternative approach is with a white painted rock lying between the two arms of the 'Y' and in line with the NW corner of the disused lifeboat house. A few visitors.

Little Porth Warna, Great Porth Warna, Little Porth Askin and Porth Askin
49°53'·20N 06°20'·75W
Sheltered WNW–N–NE–E–SE

A series of small coves where it is possible to anchor in settled weather, but which have a difficult approach and there are many rocks near the anchorages. Enter on an E heading passing 200m to S of Long Point and just N of Western Rock. Anchor in 2m sand and rock.

Eastern Isles

The Eastern Isles are a group of eleven islands and numerous rocks that are situated to the SE and S of St Martin's. The largest island, Great Ganilly, has an area of 13 hectares and is 800m long, its highest point being 32m. The islands are deserted, but they form an interesting cruising area in settled weather for skilled navigators. The area is shallow and there are numerous isolated rocks, but entry and anchorage by fin-keel vessels is possible.

Distinctive features
Great Ganilly, which has its highest hill (32m) on the NW end with a saddle and a lower hill (28m) at its SE end, is an important landmark which can be seen from afar. Hanjague, a steep-sided pyramid-shaped rock (19m), is another easily recognised feature. St Martin's daymark (red and white banded tower, 56m) is also important.

East Porth-Great Ganilly
49°57'·10N 06°15'·20W
Sheltered S–SW–W–NW

An anchorage in 1 to 2m sand and stones that has an approach with many isolated rocks. Hanjague on a stern bearing of 054° leads through, but very close to the rocks. Deserted.

West Porth-Great Ganilly
49°57'·00N 06°15'·50W
Sheltered SW–W–NW–N–NE–E

An anchorage in 1 to 2m sand, well protected but exposed at HW to W. From Crow Sound anchorage and on a course of 080°, locate Biggal rock (1m). This rock is 300m to SSE of Great Arthur; leave it 200m to port and continue on this course. Finally, when 100m from Great Ganilly, follow the coast at 100m on a NW course and thence to West Porth. There is a safer deep-water anchorage (5m sand) 300m to N of Ragged Island, but this is more exposed to NW winds. Deserted.

Arthur Porth
49°56'·67N 06°15'·75W
Sheltered SW–W–NW–N

An anchorage in 1·5m sand lying between Great and Little Arthur, with several rocks near its entrance which require care. Approach Ragged Island on a N course and when 50m from it turn to a W heading and enter the anchorage with care. Deserted.

Middle Arthur
49°56'·70N 06°16'·10W
Sheltered SW–W–NW–N–NE–E

An anchorage in 2m sand and weed off Arthur Quay. Approach with care on a N course from between Little Ganinick and Great Arthur. Deserted.

IV. History and facilities

St Agnes and Gugh

The two small islands of St Agnes and Gugh (pronounced like 'new') together measure roughly one mile each way and make up an area of 148 hectares. They are linked by a sand bar – The Bar – which usually covers at HW. Apart from two holiday dwellings near the beach, Gugh is uninhabited, while St Agnes has a permanent population of about 70 people, who are mostly engaged in flower-growing and tourism.

It is easy to walk round Gugh in an hour and worth it for the panoramic views and the sense of antiquity and remoteness. There are several prehistoric remains, which are not always obvious among the heather: the most notable are Obadiah's Barrow, a stone tomb from the Bronze Age, and a nine-foot standing stone or monolith, known as the Old Man of Gugh. In early summer, gulls nest along the shore, apparently oblivious to the gaze of humans.

After the ruggedness of Gugh, St Agnes seems relatively civilised, with its neat cottages in the three settlements of Higher, Middle and Lower Towns, and a chequerboard of flower fields, protected by high hedges of pittosporum, hebe and tamarisk. The flower farms are concentrated round the disused lighthouse, one of the oldest in Britain. This was built in 1680, but was eventually superseded by the Bishop Rock lighthouse beyond the Western Rocks (see page 61) and then, in 1911, by the Peninnis light on St Mary's. The structure on St Agnes is now kept whitewashed as a daymark – a most important one, given its position.

In the days when the St Agnes light was fuelled by coal, it was sometimes alleged that the fire was deliberately neglected in order to mislead ships and attract lucrative wrecks. The power of bringing in ships was also attributed to St Warna, an Irish saint who, according to legend, landed at the cove of the same name. Perhaps it is not surprising that the people of St Agnes were known as 'Turks' and were supposedly of swarthy appearance through interbreeding with foreign sailors. Whatever their reputation, the men were unrivalled throughout Scilly for their pilotage skills.

A concrete road, completed by the islanders themselves in the 1960s, leads to Periglis on the NW coast. The nineteenth-century church here was built on the site of an earlier one that had been funded from the proceeds of salvage. The name Periglis may be derived from the Celtic words for church and port, and indeed the bay – a drying harbour – is used by local boats. The former lifeboat house

Periglis   Old lighthouse   Peninnis Head light (St Mary's)   St Warna's Cove

St Agnes, aerial view looking ExN

stands at the top of the slipway; it was closed in 1920, but remains a testament to the many rescues organised from this strategically placed island at the SW extremity of Britain.

St Agnes and Gugh have always been isolated, even from the rest of the Isles of Scilly. In the distant past, the northern islands formed a single landmass, before this was 'drowned' by the sea and assumed its present shape in about 700 AD, while St Agnes and Gugh and Annet remained separate. The twelfth-century name for St Agnes seems to support this theory: it was Hagenes, which may be translated as 'apart island'.

Facilities

Landing places On The Bar at The Cove; on beach below Turk's Head at Porth Conger, keeping clear of jetty.

Refuse Large white bin (unmarked) on right at top of path from beach, just before road.

WCs Public lavatories by jetty in Porth Conger.

Phones Payphone at Turk's Head; phone box between Higher Town and Middle Town.

Post office and shop Near Middle Town. PO offers currency exchange for French visitors, cheque encashment, girobank, *poste restante*; faxes may be sent and received (☎ 01720 423244). Shop has range of provisions, including frozen and vegetarian food, wines, postcards, guide books; bread is usually in short supply, unless specially reserved; advance orders by fax are welcome.

Eating out Covean Cottage (licensed) – breakfast, evening meal, takeaway; Rose Cottage – coffee, tea, light lunch (both in Higher Town); Turk's Head pub above Porth Conger.

Ferries From Porth Conger quay, regular service to St Mary's in season, plus trips to other islands.

Church C of E at Lower Town, above Periglis.

Tresco

The island of Tresco is the second largest in Scilly (after St Mary's), being about two miles long by half a mile across and covering an area of 297 hectares. The permanent population is approximately 130, much augmented by a regular influx of visitors throughout the year, who stay in holiday cottages, the hotel or the inn. The whole island is a private estate, leased from the Duchy of Cornwall by the Dorrien Smith family.

For yachtsmen, Tresco offers one of the best all-weather anchorages in Scilly, at New Grimsby Sound. Cromwell's Castle guards the northern entrance to the channel and is a distinctive landmark on the shoreline, whether one is arriving from seaward or from the S. The castle was built around 1651, soon after the defeat of a Royalist uprising in the islands, led by Sir John Grenville; it was intended as a demonstration of strength by the Parliamentarian government, as well as a defence against the Dutch. This fortification replaced King Charles's Castle on the hill above, which had been constructed in the 1550s, but was so poorly sited that its guns were powerless to protect the sound. A satellite fort of the castle, The Old Blockhouse, overlooks Old Grimsby Harbour on the other side of the island and is a fine vantage-point from which to survey the approaches to that anchorage.

The northern part of the island, with its tracts of exposed heathland and outcrops of granite, is an untamed landscape, accessible only by rough paths. Nevertheless, there is evidence of ancient cairns, earthworks and settlements. There is also a hidden cave and freshwater pool, Piper's Hole, on the NE coast.

Bicycles are the main form of transport, together with tractors and buggies for visitors and their luggage. A road links the villages of New and Old Grimsby and Dolphin Town in between, as well as the estate buildings and the Abbey. This southern half of the island is in complete contrast to the north – verdant and low-lying, with pastures and cottage gardens, woods and lakes, and superb beaches rich in beautiful shells.

Presumably encouraged by the presence of fresh water on Tresco, Benedictine monks founded a priory close to the pools in the tenth century. They dedicated it to St Nicholas, that popular saint who is invoked by seafarers, among many other supplicants. However, the community could barely survive the harsh living conditions in the islands and the depredations of foreign marauders (over a hundred pirates were apparently executed on Tresco in 1209). The priory was gradually reduced to 'a poor cell of monks' and, by the sixteenth century, had been abandoned. The archways of the original building can be seen today in the Abbey Gardens.

It is hard to believe that these magnificent gardens and their surroundings were created out of a windswept, treeless expanse, overgrown with bramble and gorse and buffeted by salt spray and blown sand. The transformation was achieved by Augustus Smith who, in 1834, acquired the lease of Scilly and the title of Lord Proprietor. He decided to make his residence on Tresco, above the ruins of the priory, and immediately laid out a garden, sheltered at first by the old walls and then by the trees and windbreaks that he planted. His collection of sub-tropical plants became famous in his own lifetime and has remained one of the principal attractions of Tresco (see page 67). Within the garden, at Valhalla, he established a fascinating museum of figureheads and other relics taken from ships wrecked around the coasts of Scilly.

Augustus not only changed the face of Tresco, but he revolutionized the existence of the islanders throughout Scilly, rescuing them from the poverty into which they had fallen through the neglect of previous administrators. He reformed the system of land tenure, tackled the problem of smuggling, promoted the shipbuilding industry, removed rocks from the channel between Tresco and Bryher to make it more navigable, persuaded the farmers to grow better varieties of potatoes, and introduced

The W side of Tresco, seen from Bryher at LW

Old Grimsby Harbour (Tresco)

compulsory education 40 years ahead of mainland Britain. There is still a flourishing school at New Grimsby – a nice tribute to his endeavours – while the church of St Nicholas was built in 1882 in his memory.

Augustus was succeeded in 1874 by his nephew, Algernon Dorrien Smith, who continued his good work, both in the garden, where he added the major windbreaks, and in other spheres. Like his uncle, he realized that the mild climate of Scilly (with only a 10°C variation in the mean monthly temperature) could be exploited commercially. He therefore encouraged his tenants to plant shelter belts and, at his own expense, imported thousands of bulbs for them to grow. By the end of the nineteenth century,

the cut-flower trade was flourishing and has made an important contribution to the economy of Scilly ever since.

Facilities
Moorings 16 at New Grimsby, 6 at Old Grimsby.
Landing places On beach at New Grimsby, avoiding quay and steps; on beach at Old Grimsby – do not use quay or long causeway, which is private property of Island Hotel.
Harbourmaster Mr Henry Birch, ☎ 422792, mobile 0378 601237. May be contacted through estate office on S side of bay of New Grimsby.
Water In containers from tap near Quay Shop, New Grimsby.
Fuel Petrol in cans from estate office.
Refuse Rubbish cart near post office, New Grimsby; dustbins at root of quay, Old Grimsby.

Showers At New Inn, above New Grimsby, with use of swimming pool included in price; open 1000–1800.

WCs Public toilets behind Quay Shop, New Grimsby.

Phones Phone box by village hall, at top of hill between New and Old Grimsby; payphone at New Inn.

Post office At Quay Shop, New Grimsby, open 1200–1500 Monday to Friday; faxes may be sent and received.

Bank None, but cheques may be cashed, with bank guarantee card, at estate office.

Shop Tresco Stores, New Grimsby, open 0830–1800 Monday to Saturday, 0930–1300 Sunday. Fish, meat (fresh and frozen), vegetables, groceries, ice, newspapers, wine and spirits; credit cards accepted.

Laundry Service washes at estate office, charged per 10lb load and ready for same day collection if brought in by 1000 that morning (no underwired bras allowed!).

Eating out Quay Shop tearooms – coffee, tea, sandwiches, takeaway; New Inn – bar food, restaurant meals; Abbey Gardens café; Island Hotel, Old Grimsby.

Bicycle Hire at estate office.

Church St Nicholas C of E at Dolphin Town.

Ferries Daily from quays at New and Old Grimsby to St Mary's, often via Bryher or St Martin's; exact times depend on tide and are posted previous day on notice-boards.

Communications Direct helicopter flights to Penzance, 20 minutes (except Sunday).

Attractions Abbey Gardens and Valhalla, open daily 1000-1600.

Bryher

The smallest of the inhabited Isles of Scilly, Bryher (pronounced 'briar') measures one and a half miles long by roughly half a mile wide. Its total area, including the deserted islet of Gweal close offshore, is 133 hectares and the population numbers about 65.

Bryher takes its name from the Celtic for 'big' and 'hill' and is relatively elevated for such a notoriously low archipelago as Scilly. Watch Hill (43m), with its stone daymark, the flatter Shipman Head Down (39m) to the N, and rounded Samson Hill (40m) at the S end are all distinctive features useful for navigation. So too is the pyramidal Hangman Island, off the NE coast, which is easy to recognize in the approaches to New Grimsby Sound - especially when it has a gallows on top!

The people of Bryher, who were known as 'Thorns', were supposed to be lop-sided in their actions, perhaps because they were always leaning into the wind which sweeps in from the Atlantic. The exposed NW coast offers dramatic scenery at Hell Bay, and most of the island is open heathland, wild and lonely, with spectacular views from the

Shipman Head (Bryher), seen from King Charles Castle (Tresco)

height of Watch Hill. There are many prehistoric remains, in the form of chamber tombs on Samson Hill and Gweal Hill, a prominent burial mound on Shipman Head Down, where boulder walls link the cairns, and a submerged field system at Green Bay on the E coast.

This sheltered side of the island was chosen, not surprisingly, as a place of settlement by more recent inhabitants. The small village called The Town is situated above New Grimsby Sound and has two quays: the one of granite, by the church, can be used only at high water, while the new wooden jetty at the Bar further N is accessible at all stages of the tide and was constructed in three days, thanks to the BBC TV programme, 'Challenge Anneka'. Bryher prides itself on operating a year-round, inter-island launch service.

The church of All Saints, near the main quay, was dedicated in 1742 and later enlarged. Like the school, which closed in 1972, it originally served both Bryher and the neighbouring island of Samson to the S. The church overlooks Green Bay, a drying anchorage frequented by shoal-draught yachts. At the S tip of the island is Rushy Bay, a pretty beach with safe bathing.

Today, the residents of Bryher are mainly engaged in tourism. Holiday accommodation is varied but limited and, in the season, the locals move out to their greenhouses and garden sheds to make space for the visitors. As in the rest of Scilly, the tourist trade has replaced the traditional occupations of pilotage, salvage and rescue, at which the men of Bryher excelled. One of the most famous – and most profitable – incidents occurred in 1910, when the liner *Minnehaha* grounded on Scilly Rock, W of the island. Gigs from Bryher, including the *Czar*, brought passengers and crew and the live cargo of

Hangman I. joined to Bryher at LW, opposite Cromwell's Castle (Tresco)

cattle to safety, while the rest of the cargo was jettisoned and found its way on to the shores of Bryher. The *Czar* is still owned by the same Bryher families who commissioned her in 1879 and participates in the weekly gig races.

Facilities
Landing places Anywhere in Green Bay or on beach below The Town, but keep clear of quay and jetty.
Chandlery Blue Boats at top of jetty.
WCs Public toilets near church.
Phones Phone box in The Town.
Post office and shop Bryher Stores, Norrard, advertised with word 'shop' spelled out in signal flags. Well stocked grocery and off-licence, specializing in home-baked bread, pasties and pies.
Eating out Vine Farm Café, The Town; Fraggle Rock Café (licensed), Norrard – both do lunches, teas, evening meals, snacks; Hell Bay Hotel, by pool on W coast – coffee, tea, bar food, breakfast and dinner in restaurant.
Church All Saints C of E above Green Bay.
Ferries Regular inter-island service from church quay, below The Town, and from Bar jetty at LW.

St Helen's
St Helen's, with an area of 20 hectares, is a smooth rounded hill (42m), covered in grass and heather.

On the S shore, the ruins of a chapel mark the earliest recorded Christian building in Scilly. St Elidius lived here as a hermit in the tenth century and gave his name, in corrupted form, to the island. A service is held at the site on the nearest Sunday to the saint's feast day of 8 August. Nearby are the remains of a pest house, built in the mid-eighteenth century, which was used to quarantine disease-ridden seamen arriving from abroad. In those days, before the advent of steamships, the Isles were a major port of call for sailing vessels and St Helen's Pool itself was an alternative anchorage to St Mary's.

From the top of St Helen's, one can look across to the distinctive jagged peaks of Men-a-Vaur and to the lighthouse on Round Island. This white tower (55m) was constructed in 1887, at the expense of the resident colony of puffins, which were frightened off when the workmen began collecting their eggs for food.

St Helen's Gap, aerial view towards Tresco.

St Martin's and Tean

Some two miles long but no more than half a mile across, St Martin's is a long narrow island with a central ridge of granite. Together with White Island off the N coast, to which it is attached at LW, it forms an area of 237 hectares. It has a population of about 110, concentrated in the grandly named Higher, Middle and Lower Towns.

For yachtsmen, the most conspicuous feature of the island is the daymark (56m) on St Martin's Head, at the E tip. This 20-foot high, hollow tower was constructed in 1683 (not 1637 as inscribed) and was originally painted white. However, confusion with the St Agnes lighthouse led to at least one shipwreck in the vicinity and, in 1891, its livery was changed to the alternate red and white bands of today.

The headland and nearby Chapel Down offer splendid views across Scilly, and particularly of the Eastern Isles to the S and of the Seven Stones reef to the NE. A lightship has been maintained near the reef since 1841, but unfortunately it did not prevent the infamous disaster of the tanker *Torrey Canyon*, which steamed on to the rocks in 1967 while trying to take a short cut round Land's End.

In clear conditions, it is possible to see the mainland too. One can easily imagine how, in a far-distant age before sea levels rose, the land did not end at Land's End but extended to Scilly via the Seven Stones. There is ample evidence that the sea has continued to encroach in relatively recent times. For instance, at Par Beach in Higher Town Bay, on the S side of the island, submerged fields are shown by the remains of stone walls, visible below the high-tide line.

As the easternmost point of Scilly, St Martin's seems to have been the landfall for the earliest settlers. The first arrived from Cornwall in about 2000 BC and lived largely on a diet of limpets, according to excavations on English Island (now more shoal than island), off the SE coast. They left numerous burial chambers and field systems throughout St Martin's, as well as the oldest known statue in Britain, which now stands on a cairn on Chapel Down. House foundations and pieces of pottery have also been discovered at Par Beach, dating from the later, Romano-British period, although the most important find was at Nornour, SE of English Island (see page 62). Finally, the sixteenth century saw a further influx to St Martin's of people from Sennen in Cornwall and gave the inhabitants their supposed characteristics of red or sandy hair and blue eyes.

The island can be explored on foot in a convenient circuit, which highlights the contrast between the rugged N coast, with its spectacular rock-strewn bays, and the gentler S side, sloping down to shallow waters of an incredible blue. Above the beaches, fields have been hedged in to take advantage of the light, sandy soil, and these sun-traps produce the earliest flowers in Scilly. In addition to bulb-growing, the islanders catch fish, especially lobster and crab. However, tourism has become their chief occupation, with a hotel, campsite and holiday homes to accommodate visitors.

In the eighteenth century, the kelp industry flourished. Kelp, an ingredient in the manufacture of iodine, soap and glass, was produced by burning seaweed in special pits, examples of which survive on White Island. Much of the seaweed was gathered on Tean, where families from St Martin's would move for the summer; the ruins of their cottages can still be seen. This little island of 16 hectares was also used for grazing cattle in the past. Today, it is barren and deserted except for seabirds, notably ringed plover and tern. During their breeding season from April to July, there is a voluntary restriction on landing on Tean.

Facilities
Moorings 7 in Tean Sound; contact St Martin's on the Isle Hotel, ☎ 422092, or through local boat *Voyager*.
Landing places 3 quays – at Lower Town, near St Martin's on the Isle Hotel; Higher Town, E of Cruther's Hill (dries at LW); and Old Quay, W of Cruther's Hill (dries at half tide) – but best to avoid these and use adjacent beaches.
Water In containers from hotel.
Refuse Rubbish disposal at hotel (separated into glass, cans and burnable items).
Showers At hotel.
Phones Phone boxes in Middle and Higher Towns; payphone at hotel.
Post office At St Martin's general stores, Higher Town.
Shops General stores, Higher Town – frozen food and off-licence, newspapers to order, open 0900–1230 and 1330–1730 Monday to Saturday, 1000–1100 Sunday; Lindy's Locker, Lower Town – fruit and vegetables
Eating out Polreath Guest House, Higher Town (licensed) – tea, lunch, draught real ale; Seven Stones pub, open 1100–1700 and 1930–2230 Monday to Saturday, 1200–14.00 Sunday; Little Arthur café, Higher Town; St Martin's on the Isle Hotel.
Church C of E near Higher Town.
Ferries Regular service from Lower Town and Higher Town quays to St Mary's and other islands.

St Martin's Hotel   St Martin's daymark

St Martin's looking E

St Martin's Hotel   *Quay*   *Bab's Carn*   *Southward Carn*   *Tean*

St Martin's, looking across Tean Sound

St Martin's Bay   *Round I. light*   *White I.*

The N side of St Martin's, seen from Chapel Down

Samson

Samson is about three quarters of a mile long and 39 hectares in area, making it the largest of the deserted islands. The twin rounded hills (33m and 40m), joined by a low sandy isthmus, are unmistakable landmarks from most directions.

Humans were present on the island from prehistoric times, as evidenced by burial chambers and hut circles on the hills and, on the shore, traces of field walls running out to sea. More recent settlers established themselves in the S part, increasing from a single family in 1669 to 34 persons by 1822. Despite the bleak terrain, they managed to eke out a living, mainly by fishing, kelp-making and pilotage; their diet consisted of potatoes, fish and limpets.

In the early nineteenth century, the people invested in a sailing yawl, *Fly*, to supplement the piloting and salvage work previously carried out in gigs. However, both *Fly* and its larger successor, the cutter *Defiance*, broke from their moorings and were driven on to the rocks, and the venture failed. The lack of a safe harbour in Samson is something that present-day yachtsmen might bear in mind.

By the 1850s, the dwindling and increasingly ageing community on Samson had ceased to be viable and was probably near starvation. Augustus Smith, as Lord Proprietor of Scilly, ordered the evacuation of the inhabitants and rehoused them elsewhere. Only their ruined cottages and overgrown fields remain. Subsequently, Smith grazed cattle on the island and attempted to keep deer there – until they took advantage of LW and escaped across the channel to Tresco.

Western Rocks and Annet

Annet is the largest island W of St Agnes, with an area of 21 hectares. It consists of low hills linked by a saddle and has a conspicuous line of tooth-like rocks off its N tip. From Annet to the Western Rocks, a horseshoe-shaped chain of islets and rocks extends over two miles, while further outcrops, including Bishop Rock, are scattered to the extreme W and NW.

These isolated rocks and ledges, many of them partially submerged, their associated overfalls and currents, and the force of the Atlantic swell – all combine to make the waters W of Scilly especially dangerous. Among the numerous shipwrecks in the area, the worst recorded disaster happened in 1707, when a British fleet under Sir Cloudesley Shovel was returning from the siege of Toulon. Owing to a miscalculation of longitude, the fleet found itself not off Ushant but off Scilly, where the flagship *Association* struck the Gilstone and three other ships sank. Over 1,600 men were lost and the body of the Admiral, who was subsequently given a state funeral, was washed ashore on the SE coast of St Mary's.

In 1875, the Retarrier Ledges claimed the most serious wreck of the nineteenth century, the German transatlantic mail-steamer *Schiller*, which was one of the largest vessels of her day. In dense fog, she passed inside Bishop Rock and came to a violent stop; only two lifeboats were successfully launched from the stricken ship and, out of a total complement of 372 people, there were just 37 survivors. Another casualty of huge size was the seven-masted schooner *Thomas W. Lawson*, the biggest sailing ship ever built. En route from Philadelphia to London in 1907, she was driven on to the Outer Ranneys, W of Annet, and broke up, shedding her cargo of crude oil; 16 of the 18 crew died, together with the St Agnes pilot, who had gone to help.

South Hill   Castle Bryher   North Hill   Scilly Rock   Gweal

Samson, looking NW from Star Castle Hotel (St Mary's)

Looking SW across Smith Sound from Star Castle Hotel (St Mary's)

The lighthouse on Bishop Rock was already in operation when these two tragedies occurred, having been first lit in 1858. Situated on a small ridge of rock that rises sheer from the depths, the initial iron structure was started in 1847 but swept away in a storm in 1850. It was replaced by a tower built of granite, which was quarried in Cornwall, dressed on Rat Island, St Mary's, and then shipped to the site. During the six years it took to complete the lighthouse, the construction workers lived in huts on Rosevear and even managed to grow their own vegetables. In the 1880s, the tower was reinforced, the height was raised, making it the tallest lighthouse in the British Isles at 44m, and a new light was installed, which could – and can – be seen from 24 miles away.

Colonies of seabirds inhabit the islands; Annet is a sanctuary for puffins, as well as the elusive storm petrel and Manx shearwater, and is closed to visitors between 15 April and 20 August. Grey seals also breed in the area, particularly on the Western Rocks. These rocks are 'the most wave-exposed found in England and Wales and are therefore considered to be of national importance', being designated a Special Area within the Isles of Scilly Marine Park.

Eastern Isles

The Eastern Isles consist of 11 islands and numerous rocks, situated to the SE and S of St Martin's. The largest island, Great Ganilly, covers an area of 13 hectares and is an important landmark, with a hill (32m and 28m) at each end of a central saddle. Hanjague (19m), a steep-sided pyramid, is also easily recognized, as is the St Martin's daymark.

Sheltered from the W, the Eastern Isles benefit from more soil and grass than many of the deserted islands. Their attractive scenery, together with wild flowers, seabirds and seals, make them a popular destination for daytrippers, brought by local launches. The island of Nornour, which can be reached by crossing the rocky bar from Great Ganilly at LW, is of particular interest. It is the site of an ancient village, where a remarkable collection of Roman jewellery and artefacts was discovered; many of these finds can be seen in the St Mary's Museum.

In settled weather, the Eastern Isles offer several delightful anchorages for experienced yachtsmen, but are only recommended for a daytime stop.

St Mary's

The largest of the Isles of Scilly, St Mary's covers an area of 629 hectares; it measures about two and a half miles across at its widest point and has a coastline of 9 to 10 miles. There are approximately 1,500 permanent inhabitants – four fifths of the total population of Scilly – plus something like 100,000 visitors a year, either passing through or staying on the island.

St Mary's also has the highest land in the archipelago at Telegraph (48m) on the NW side, marked by the 15m-high, grey, round telegraph tower. Beyond this, in a line to the NNW, are the tall, latticework TV tower (119m), which has a solid white section on top, and three radio masts, again of latticework and sometimes difficult to distinguish. On the E coast, a white-painted wind generator is a conspicuous feature, while to the S the masts and control tower of the airport are noticeable. The lighthouse at the S tip, on Peninnis Head, is small and not very prominent, and it can be easily confused with the old St Agnes light when approaching from the E.

Hugh Town is the administrative capital of Scilly, the commercial centre and the port for connections with both the mainland and the off-islands. It takes its name from the 'hugh' or 'hoe' on which it is situated, meaning a promontory or, in this case, a narrow sandbar, dividing Porth Cressa from St Mary's Pool. The harbour itself is privately run by the Duchy of Cornwall, which has owned the Isles of Scilly since 1337, although most of Hugh Town is now freehold property.

Originally known as Ennor, St Mary's had its first capital at Old Town in the S of the island and a castle, dating from the thirteenth century, nearby. In the reign of Elizabeth I, the focus began to shift to Hugh Town. The queen ordered the construction of a new castle on Garrison Hill, to serve as a defence against Spain and a protection from privateers. This fortress, in the shape of an eight-sided star, was completed in 1593–4 and was followed by the building of the harbour quay in 1601. The quay was subsequently extended to Rat Island and further seaward in the nineteenth century, allowing access at all stages of the tide and providing a more effective breakwater.

Star Castle is an important landmark, though not always an obvious one from seaward, and its ramparts afford a fine all-round view of the islands. During the Civil War, it was a Royalist stronghold and a staging-post for the future Charles II in 1646 on his way to exile in France. The Royalists, led by Sir John Grenville, controlled the castle and the surrounding seas for three years; they were finally forced to surrender in 1651, when Parliamentarian forces under Admiral Blake landed on Tresco and imposed a blockade. In the eighteenth century, a curtain wall was added to the castle, but the military establishment was gradually reduced. In 1933, Star Castle became a hotel, which it has continued to be.

Hugh Town today is a real little town, the only one in Scilly, with many facilities and much activity, particularly when the ferry arrives. A weekly service to Penzance was started in the early nineteenth century by the Tregarthen brothers, owners of the hotel of that name. In 1920, the islanders founded the Isles of Scilly Steamship Company and the first *Scillonian*, carrying passengers, cargo and mail, was launched soon afterwards. In those days, when a permanent watch was kept at the coastguard station on Telegraph, a black ball would be hoisted up the mast, to indicate that the ferry had left the mainland; the ball was dropped when she came into sight, thus warning the local taxi-drivers, hoteliers and shopkeepers to prepare for visitors. The present *Scillonian III* was commissioned in 1977, while the *Gry Maritha* was purchased in 1989 to handle additional freight.

Although sometimes overshadowed by the attractions of the other islands, St Mary's has its own special charm (a fact no doubt appreciated by the former prime minister, Harold Wilson, who made his holiday home here in the 1960s). Heathery downs, marshes and pools, lush valleys and woods, bulb fields enclosed by hedges, pretty coves and beaches – all compose a varied landscape, and one that is easily explored on foot.

Peninnis Head, reached by the coastal path, provides a stark contrast to this otherwise gentle scene. The cliffs and rocks have been carved by the weather into weird shapes, which have been given fanciful names such as Tooth Rock and Laughing Man. In geological terms, they are excellent examples of the vertical and horizontal decomposition of granite. The automatic Peninnis light, an insignificant-looking structure but a vital aid to navigation, was installed in 1911.

For lovers of history, St Mary's has several important ancient sites, many of them maintained by English Heritage. At Halangy Down, on the NW coast near Telegraph, is a village of round houses, which dates from about the second century BC and was still in use in Roman times. S of the settlement is the 3,000-year old burial chamber of Bant's Carn, which is thought to have been an ancestral shrine. (The location of Bant's Carn is correctly shown on the Ordnance Survey map, but incorrectly on the Admiralty chart). Further tombs are to be found at

Porth Cressa   Hugh Town   Peninnis Head light

St Mary's, aerial view looking N

Watermill Cove (St Mary's)

Innisidgen, on the other side of Telegraph, at Porth Hellick Down, on the E shore, and on Buzza Hill, above Hugh Town. The squat Buzza Tower, which is a reference mark when approaching St Mary's harbour from sea, was originally a Martello tower and later a windmill. The tower on Telegraph was also constructed against a possible French invasion. In 1814, it acquired a semaphore, for sending signals to the mainland. This was the only direct means of communication until, in 1902, as a result of experiments conducted there by Marconi, a radio mast was erected and a coastguard station established, one of the earliest to be equipped with wireless telegraphy.

The E coast of St Mary's is designated a Special Area within the Isles of Scilly Marine Park, on account of its sponges, corals and sea fans, which are not only rare but slow-growing and easily damaged. Watermill Cove is a delightful little anchorage, well sheltered from the SW and with a sandy beach at LW. In the eighteenth century, it had a quay for the export of kelp, the product of burning seaweed, which was done in special pits on Toll's Island. Pelistry Bay is a popular picnic spot with a large, secluded beach, although currents make swimming hazardous when the bar between island and shore is covered.

Porth Hellick, to the S, is the bay where the body of Sir Cloudesley Shovel was washed ashore in 1707 (see page 60). A rough-hewn monument commemorates the event. Continuing past the airport, which was completed at the beginning of the second world war and replaced the landing strip on the golf course, one reaches Old Town. The church is the remnant of a much larger, Norman edifice and was renovated in 1891. By then, however, it had been superseded by the new church in Hugh Town, built in 1838, which Augustus Smith was required to provide under the terms of his lease as Lord

Proprietor. In Old Town churchyard are buried over a hundred victims of another famous wreck, that of the *Schiller* in 1875 (see page 60).

The road leads directly back to Hugh Town, conveniently passing the excellent museum, or a diversion can be taken to Porth Cressa, which is a useful alternative anchorage to St Mary's Pool, especially in a NW wind. This, together with Town Beach opposite, was once the centre of the shipbuilding industry, which enjoyed a brief boom with the encouragement of Augustus Smith. By the 1850s, there were four yards at work, but thirty years later they had all closed, unable to compete with the latest technology of iron, steam-driven vessels.

Facilities
Moorings 38 in St Mary's Pool.
Landing places Visitors' dinghy park clearly marked below steps at junction of New Quay and Old Quay – do not use main quay or steps along it because of constant traffic from ferry, launches and other vessels; on Town Beach and on beach at Porth Cressa.
Harbourmaster Mr Jeff Penhaligon. Harbour Office next to hotel on quay, open daily 0700–1900. Call sign St Mary's Harbour on VHF Ch 16, working channel 14. Address: Harbour Office, The Quay, Hugh Town, St Mary's, Isles of Scilly; ☎ and *Fax* 01720 422768.
Customs HM Customs, Lower Strand, ☎ 422571.
Police Station off Garrison Lane, ☎ 422444.
Chandlery Isles of Scilly Steamship Co, Hugh Street; Scillonian Marine, Strand.
Marine engineers, boat repairs Isles of Scilly Steamship Co; or inquire at Harbour Office.
Sailmakers Rat Island Sail Locker.
Weather Local weather bulletin posted daily outside Harbour Office at 0830 (GMT) and displayed at Tourist Information Centre, Porth Cressa.
Water Large amounts, metered, direct to vessel alongside quay, berthing by prior arrangement with HM when *Scillonian III* is not in port; containers may also be filled from a tap near Harbour Office, with HM's permission.
Fuel Sibley's Fuel and Marine Services, Rat Island, open 0800–1200, 1300–1700 weekdays, 0800–1200 Saturday; large amounts pumped direct to vessel as above. In cans from filling stations on Telegraph Road, above Porthmellon, and at Porth Cressa.
Gas Camping Gaz from Sibley's; Calor Gas from Island Supply Stores, Garrison Lane, who will deliver to quay (price includes a 36% freight charge for carriage from mainland).
Refuse Skips behind Harbour Office and on Old Quay; litter bins at Porth Cressa.
Showers In block next to Harbour Office, coin-operated, open daily 0800–1945.
WCs Public toilets in block next to Harbour Office; also at Porth Cressa and in Lower Strand.
Phones Phone box behind Harbour Office, also phone in Harbourside Hotel on quay; further phone boxes at foot of Garrison Hill and in The Parade,

St Mary's Pool in rough weather, when there is a risk of colliding with adjacent empty mooring buoys

Hugh Town.

Post office In Hugh Street, open 0815–1700 Monday to Friday, 0815–1215 Saturday. Post box on quay. HM will also keep mail, and send and receive faxes (see above).

Banks Lloyds, with cashpoint, and Barclays, both in Hugh Street, open 0900–1600 Monday to Friday.

Shops In Hugh Town – Co-op supermarket open daily 0800–2200; butchers, fishmongers, bakery, greengrocer, delicatessen; also chemist, newsagent, bookshop, film-developing, clothes, arts, crafts, gifts, souvenirs etc. Most shops open 0900–1700 Monday to Saturday; early closing Wednesday, but only out of season.

Launderette At Porth Cressa, service washes only, open 0900–1700 Monday to Saturday.

Eating out Wide selection of pubs, cafés, takeaways, restaurants and hotels in Hugh Town, Porth Cressa and Old Town.

Medical Health clinic and hospital, Hospital Lane, off Church Road – doctor, ☎ 422628; dentist, ☎ 422694; hospital, ☎ 422392.

Transport Taxis, buses, including island tours, car rental.

Bicycle hire At Porth Cressa.

Tourist information Centre at Porth Cressa, closed Sunday.

Churches C of E, Methodist and RC in Hugh Town.

Yacht club Isles of Scilly YC, Lower Strand.

Ferries Regular launches to off-islands from quay; information about pleasure trips at Old Quay.

Communications Skybus flights, ☎ 0345 105555: to Land's End (15 minutes), Newquay (30 minutes), Plymouth (45 minutes), Exeter (50 minutes), Bristol (1 hour 10 minutes) and Southampton (1 hour 30 minutes). Helicopter service to Penzance (20 minutes). *Scillonian III*, ferry to Penzance (2 hours 40 minutes), in high season daily except Sunday.

Attractions St Mary's Museum, Church Street; gig racing, Wednesday and Friday evenings, finishing at end of quay; wildlife tours, information at Old Quay – guided walks round St Mary's and other islands, looking at natural and local history.

V. Natural history

Birds

The Isles of Scilly have long been regarded as one of the best bird-watching regions in Britain. Although only about 50 species of birds actually breed on the islands, there is a wide range of migrants arriving during spring and autumn. This results in an annual total of usually about 240 species and a grand total, since records began in the nineteenth century, of over 400 different species. Moreover, many of the species on the British list were first sighted in Scilly and, in some cases, have only ever been seen there.

Seabirds account for a large proportion of the species that breed on Scilly. These include puffins on Annet, which is one of the southernmost breeding colonies, guillemots and razorbills on the outer islands and, in the summer months, terns in the low-lying areas. Razorbills and terns are often found fishing between the islands, while guillemots and puffins go further afield for their catch. Waders, on their way to and from breeding grounds further north, use the smaller rocks for roosting.

Shags far outnumber cormorants in the islands, sometimes gathering in huge flocks to follow a school of fish. In winter, the great northern diver can be seen in more sheltered waters. In summer, both the Manx shearwater and the storm petrel may be sighted offshore, with the chance of some rarer shearwaters and petrels appearing in early autumn. Gannets are present throughout the year, and in larger numbers in the autumn, when the great and Arctic skuas are occasional visitors.

The islands have become wooded only in the last hundred years or so and, therefore, few woodland birds have reached Scilly. Woodpeckers are very rare, as are owls, treecreepers, jays and magpies, most having been recorded less than ten times. On the other hand, some birds have benefited from the hedges surrounding the flower fields, resulting in one of the highest concentrations of wren and song thrush in Britain, with robin, dunnock and blackbird not far behind.

Since most species are migrants, they can appear in unexpected places and it is not unusual to find land birds along the shore or waders foraging in the fields. However, there are favoured sites for certain species on each island. On St Mary's, there are two nature trails from the Lower and Higher Moors to Porth Hellick, which lead through marshes and past small pools; here swallows and martins are often observed, while warblers frequent the sallows and reeds nearby. The beaches around Hugh Town are excellent for shore birds, with turnstone, sanderling and oystercatcher in evidence most months, except during midsummer. The stonechat and rock pipit populate the strand line all year and are joined after the breeding season by the black redstart, chiffchaff and pied wagtail. The headlands around the island echo to the familiar call of the cuckoo, from late April until the end of June.

With the two largest lakes in Scilly and a substantial wooded area, Tresco is a unique island. The lakes attract a wide range of waterfowl during the winter months and have small breeding populations of tufted duck and gadwall. The surrounding trees and bushes are favoured by migrant flycatchers, warblers and other woodland birds, including such unusual species as golden oriole in the spring and yellow-browed warbler and red-breasted flycatcher in the autumn. In complete contrast is the rugged marine heath of Castle Down, in the N of Tresco, where wheatears, larks and pipits abound.

St Agnes is the most exposed of the major islands, bearing as it does the brunt of the SW winds, and its small patchwork fields with their tall hedges are a haven for tired migrants. Over the years, many very rare birds have stopped on this tiny island and more American vagrants have been recorded here than anywhere else in the UK. The beaches around the pool are among the best places in Scilly for observing waders, with redshank, greenshank, grey plover and purple sandpiper besides the more common species. In autumn, if the water level drops enough to expose some mud, the pool is also a good area for freshwater waders. The nearby cricket pitch is frequented by linnets, wheatears, pipits and the occasional rarity such as the short-toed lark or the hoopoe. In the S and W of the island, the open headlands have yet another range of birds: whimbrels are often seen on the short heather during the spring migration and sometimes, if the winds are in the W in the autumn, dotterels and American waders.

Because of its shape, the long, thin island of St Martin's produces an updraught, which is favoured by birds of prey and by the one pair of ravens known to be resident. Although the kestrel is the only bird of prey to breed regularly, peregrine, sparrowhawk and merlin are noted most months outside the breeding season, with harriers and kites recorded regularly. Chapel Down, on the E end of the island, has a small colony of breeding fulmars and some of the larger gulls breeding close by. The heathland here often yields the first Lapland and snow buntings of the autumn in September. In early summer, the northern slopes of the island are a haunt of cuckoos and stonechats, while in autumn many pipits and skylarks populate The Plains, where they may be disturbed by a passing kestrel or merlin. On the S side, the flower fields attract a great variety of migrants. The elms near the cricket pitch at Higher Town are a good site for insect-eating birds, such as warblers and flycatchers. Finally, the sand flats S of Middle Town can hold huge numbers of ringed plovers and sanderlings, especially in winter.

Bryher, with its spectacular views, offers the least shelter on the islands for foraging birds, but it still has much of interest. The open heaths, for instance, are popular with migrant ring ouzels. Any sunny hedge is worth watching for insect-catching birds and Bryher seems to do particularly well for the scarce icterine and melodious warblers during August and September. The neighbouring island of Samson has a large colony of lesser black-backed gulls and a small colony of kittiwakes nesting on the low cliffs. The sandy areas to the W are good spots to look for curlew, redshank, greenshank and the odd godwit.

Amateur or expert, the visitor who is interested in birds can find much to enjoy in Scilly.

Animals

Although the islands do not have many resident animals, they do boast one of the rarest in Britain. This is the lesser white-toothed shrew, known locally as the Scilly shrew, a tiny creature which is found throughout Scilly, but can be very difficult to spot. The Atlantic grey seal breeds on the smaller outer rocks during the early autumn, when the pups may occasionally be seen, and is also present on the Eastern Isles.

Brown rats, rabbits and house and field mice inhabit all the major islands. Frogs are on St Martin's and St Mary's, and slow worms have recently been released on Bryher. Hedgehogs have been introduced on St Mary's in the last twenty years and pipistrelle bats still survive in small numbers on the inhabited islands. At sea, harbour porpoise, several species of dolphin and the occasional whale are recorded most years, as well as basking shark.

Only a small number of butterflies breed on Scilly. Some of these, such as the meadow brown, common blue and speckled wood, have developed distinct sub-species on the islands. Migrant species like the red admiral and small tortoiseshell appear in huge numbers in some years, with the clouded yellow and painted lady being less common but also prone to having 'boom' years. Other migrant insects include some dragonflies, of which migrant hawkers are the most numerous, to such an extent that they may now be breeding. Among resident insects are common darters and some damselflies.

Flowers

The flora of the islands is very varied, with a range of habitats including coast and heath, hedgerow, ditch and marsh, stone walls, fields and wasteground. Many of the plants on Scilly are common in Cornwall and SW Britain, but there are several that are unknown on the mainland. A large number of plants are escapes from cultivation, mostly aliens from the Mediterranean, South Africa and South America, which may have been introduced through shipping, while others are former commercial crops that have become naturalized.

A few species occur on the islands right on the edge of their range. The dwarf pansy, for instance, is known in the UK only from Scilly and the Channel Islands, the nearest colonies being on the Atlantic seaboard of southern France. The flower-farming system means that the fields are left alone for most of the spring and this encourages wildflowers to grow in profusion. Thus, the Bermuda buttercup turns the fields yellow during late April and early May, while the ubiquitous three-cornered leek invades almost every garden.

Most of the windbreak hedges originate from the southern hemisphere, notably the New Zealand pittosporum, which is the most efficient. Coprosma, olearia and hebe, from the same country, are also used, together with euonymus from Japan and escallonia from Chile. The commonest deciduous tree is the native British elm, which has so far escaped the destructive Dutch elm disease. Shelter belts of Monterey and lodge pole pines criss-cross many of the islands, although the former are being replaced because they are less resilient to winter gales.

A walk along the cliffs in early summer will reveal masses of thrift, birdsfoot trefoil, English stonecrop and foxgloves; like many red- or pink-flowered plants on Scilly, the foxglove is usually a much darker colour than its mainland counterpart. The Hottentot fig or ice plant, from South Africa, carpets large areas. It belongs to the mesembryanthemum family, of which several members are now regarded as naturalized on the islands.

Scilly is always associated with the daffodil, which is grown as a commercial crop. Many varieties of daffodil and Tazetta narcissus have escaped from the fields and grow wild in the hedgerows, where they tend to flower in early spring after the peak of the winter picking season. Other commercial escapes include iris and whistling jacks – a purple gladiolus – flowering in early summer, followed by agapanthus and amaryllis in late summer.

Basic checklists for the birds and flowers of Scilly can be obtained from the Isles of Scilly Environmental Trust, Hugh Town, St Mary's.

Tresco Abbey Gardens

Once described as 'Kew Gardens with the lid off', Tresco Abbey Gardens contain a range of exotic plants that is unrivalled in the British Isles, if not the world. Thanks to the unique climatic conditions of Tresco, the gardens are very rarely affected by temperatures below freezing; at the same time, they benefit from warm air currents produced by the Gulf Stream and from constant high humidity created by the sea. Shelter, however, is the final essential ingredient and, for this reason, the gardens are surrounded by windbreaks to protect them from the savage, salt-laden gales of winter. All these factors enable an extraordinary collection of plants to flourish.

To visit Tresco Abbey Gardens is to visit not one garden but many. South Africa, Australia, New Zealand, South America, Mexico, California, the Canary Islands and Madeira are but a few of the regions represented by the plants growing here, with the emphasis on the southern hemisphere. The gardens extend to an area of little over 20 acres and are arranged in a series of S-facing terraces on a gentle slope, protected to the N and W by hillsides covered in conifers and evergreens.

The Top Terrace looks out over the sea towards St Agnes and St Mary's. Although exposed to the salt winds, its sun-baked soil is an ideal home for South African plants and notably for the spectacular, summer-flowering proteas (this being the most northerly place in the world where they grow outside). Descending to the Middle Terrace, through 40ft high Canary Island palms, one could easily imagine oneself in the Mediterranean. The outstanding feature, from spring onwards, is the tree echiums; also from the Canaries, these relatives of our native viper's bugloss send up tall, rocket-like spires of deep blue flowers, with variations in pink or almost red. Blue agapanthus have seeded themselves in rocky corners and succulents from many countries cling to the granite cliffs. This part of the gardens also suits the puyas which, like pineapple, belong to the bromeliad family; their huge, prickly spikes of yellow or metallic blue flowers appear in early summer and are pollinated by blackbirds on Tresco, in the absence of the hummingbirds of their native Chile.

There is very much more to see within these exciting and varied gardens. From early spring to late autumn, the visitors will be rewarded with a wealth of colour and interest and an unforgettable experience.

Index